Preaching to a Multi-generational Assembly

Preaching to a Multi-generational Assembly

Andrew Carl Wisdom, O.P.

LITURGICAL PRESS
Collegeville, Minnesota

www.litpress.org

Cover design by David Manahan, O.S.B. Photo by The Crosiers.

1 2 3 4 5 6 7 8

Library of Congress Cataloging-in-Publication Data

Wisdom, Andrew Carl, 1961–
Preaching to a multi-generational assembly / Andrew Carl Wisdom.
p. cm.
Includes bibliographical references (p.) and index.
ISBN 0-8146-2933-4
1. Catholic preaching—United States. 2. Age groups—United States.
I. Title.

BX1795.P72W57 2004
251—dc22

2003060783

Dedicated to my parents
Sue and Carl Wisdom,
whose lives bear witness to the preached Word.

Yes, Mom and Dad,

"every child comes with a message from God,"
so no generation should ever be left behind
in the preaching of the Word.

Contents

Tables and Graphs

Acknowledgments

Our achievements are never exclusively our own, but a collective tapestry. This completed tapestry is intertwined with the contributed threading of many others. Let me acknowledge those whose stitches significantly helped in this book coming together.

This book began with my Doctor of Ministry in Preaching thesis project at Aquinas Institute of Theology. I am grateful for the constant encouragement of the D.Min. Preaching faculty: Fr. Gregory Heille, O.P., Sr. Marygrace Peters, O.P., Fr. Frank Quinn, O.P., Sr. Mary Margaret Pazdan, O.P., and, in particular, Sr. Joan Delaplane, O.P., the consummate cheerleader for the program. I am especially indebted to my advisor Fr. Charles Bouchard, O.P. His critiques could not have been more clear, concise, constructive, and confidence-instilling. Nor could he have made himself any more available. Charlie's style of direction always left me feeling that he was working to support my vision of the project rather than me working to satisfy his!

Others to whom I owe a debt of gratitude include:

- Communications Professor Karla Scott, Ph.D., and Professor of Marketing Jim Fischer, Ph.D., both of St. Louis University, for their guidance of chapters two and three as well as Mike Flynn from D'Arcy Advertising for crucial advice on my research methods and instruments.

- My academic colleague and friend, Sr. Dorothy Jonaitis, O.P., whose proofreading of chapters, double-checking of my numbers and footnotes, as well as refining my graphs showed a genuine loyalty and an untiring generosity. Aquinas librarian Sally Gunter also never hesitated to help in the tedious task of grammar checking and proofing.

- My Dominican brothers of the Province of St. Albert the Great, men among whom I am proud to count myself, who have constantly offered words of encouragement. I especially want to thank my classmate, Fr. Jordan Kelly, O.P., and Fr. Louis Morrone, O.P., Fr. Michael Mascari, O.P., Fr. Rick Peddicord, O.P., Fr. Art Cavitt, O.P., Fr. Bruce Williams, O.P., and Br. Reid Perkins-Buzo, O.P., for his assistance with indexing.
- The three parishes that provided invaluable feedback as test sites for my intergenerational preaching theory and to those who coordinated the effort: Fr. Gary Braun and The Catholic Student Center at Washington University in St. Louis, Missouri; Fr. Steve Janoski and St. Jerome Parish in Troy, Illinois; and Fr. John Vien and St. Peter Parish in Kirkwood, Missouri.
- Those with whom I began this journey at the North American College nearly twenty years ago: David Kersten, Patrick McGovern, Msgr. Joseph Quinn, and Mark Pickering. The witness of their lives and the fidelity of their friendship formed my heart and mind and gave me confidence each step along the way.
- My faithful college friend, Jennifer Tompulis, and my inspirational big brother, Richard Carl, a preacher himself in the venerable tradition of John Wesley.
- My *two* Rocks of Gibraltar in life, my sisters, Christine Hallett and Carla Vaughan. No brother could ask for more unconditional love or constant presence than I have received from them.
- Finally, to my parents and friends, Sue and Carl Wisdom, to whom this book is dedicated. With eleven children, they were pioneers in the art of effective intergenerational preaching long before I put pen to paper!

Introduction

In the last couple of years, I have perceived a shift in what was needed in preaching. My perception came through some very practical laboratories: the urban and rural parishes in St. Louis and in Southern Illinois in which I preached and presided during my formation as a Dominican. As I was in a different parish each weekend, I was continually challenged to preach to vastly different social, religious, and cultural viewpoints of multi-generational assemblies. I began to take greater note of those who stopped to comment on the homily. Sometimes people were pretty much from the same generations but other times they were somewhat mixed. Several times, there was clearly an intergenerational makeup in the line.

I was also strongly influenced by generational trends within my own family. While there were obvious generational differences among us, all family members shared a fundamental belief in Christianity, a Catholic upbringing, and a common hunger, instilled by our parents, for religious authenticity. All of us shared a common parochial menu of Catholic ritual, symbols, and belief-systems and, therefore, a similar language. However, the meanings behind those Catholic symbols and practices were often appropriated in different ways. For example, the rosary with its mantra-like recitation of the Our Father and Hail Mary is an exercise in contemplation for my mother, while an imaginative gospel walk through the major events of Jesus' and Mary's lives for my twelve-year-old nephew, Andy.

A shared Catholic culture is one opportunity to bridge the individual lenses of many generations by utilizing a common language while respecting spiritual differences. Practically, this occurs when the language of the preacher reflects the interweaving of cultural, religious and linguistic symbols fundamental to each generation's self-understanding. So, what was needed in my mind was a homiletic approach that embraces a qualified sectioning of the assembly based on the subculture of generation.

> I remember a friend sharing an incident that occurred at Eucharist one Sunday morning. After the proclamation of the Gospel, his sixty-something pastor began preaching to the congregation. The assembly was positively engaged until he illustrated his point with a reference to the Angelus.[1]
>
> Startled at the blank stares from many in the congregation, he suddenly smiled understandingly and acknowledged: "You younger generations have little or no experience of the Angelus, do you?" My friend wondered: Had it not occurred to his preacher until that moment to look at his congregation from a multi-generational viewpoint?

Advocating for that multi-generational viewpoint is my primary motivation in this project. The goal was to create a credible, new homiletic model to make Catholic preaching more exciting, more accessible, and more effective for *both* the assembly and preacher by making it more generationally relevant. To that end, this work tackles four areas.

- It reflects upon the current state of preaching through Catholic and Protestant voices;
- It argues from communication theory that generation is a subculture like ethnicity and race and should be seriously considered in homiletic preparation;
- It discusses the application of contemporary market segmentation theory in preaching by proposing a qualified "generational segmentation" of the Sunday assembly;
- It applies both theories to the Catholic sacramental tradition to demonstrate both the opportunity and viability of intergenerational preaching in a Catholic context.

Let me flesh out each area in a little greater detail. Much attention over the last thirty years has been paid to developing multi-cultural

[1] Rarely used today, the *Angelus* is a traditional Catholic prayer that calls one to prayerfully pause daily at six in the morning, noon, and six in the evening to recall the Incarnation of Christ.

awareness. I believe a timely corollary exists now in the development of a multigenerational perspective. Most experts who study generational theory agree in delineating age groups along the following five categories: Builders, *The Institutional Generation* (1901–1924); The Silent Generation, *Bridge Builders* (1925–1942); Baby Boomers, *Visionaries and Seekers* (1943–1961/64); Generation-X, *A Relational Generation* (1961/64–1981)[2] and the Millennial Generation, *Young Navigators* (1981–present).[3] Varying percentages of these generations sit in our pews each weekend. What I wrestled with was how to preach the word of God in a meaningful way when *generational dialects*[4] are so diverse. "Dialects . . . have to do with boundaries. Social dialects say who we are . . . regional dialects, where we come from." Those same boundaries exist not only between social classes but also between generations. Multiple age groups have different generational mindsets and feelings as well as distinct values and characteristics.

If the Church is intergenerational by nature, understanding the linguistic relativity of words is crucial to evaluating how to effectively craft an intergenerational homily. By intergenerational, I mean ***preaching the Gospel message in a culturally relevant and life-giving manner to the four to five generations comprising the Sunday assembly, through targeted generational images, metaphors and linguistic references.*** An example of a linguistic reference is one taken from my niece Katie's generational dictionary or lexicon: "Meet me online at ten for an IM."

Before one can proclaim the Word, it is necessary for the preacher to understand the generational language use and cultural nuance of each word used. For example, words like "sacrifice" and "self-denial" are heard differently by a sixty-eight-year-old retired business executive who grew up during the Depression and a World War, and a

[2] Ronald J. Allen, "Preaching to Different Generations," *Encounter* 58, no. 4 (1997) 369–400.

[3] John Roberto, *Generations of Faith: Institute Program,* Conference Handbook, May 31–June 1, 2000, Omaha, Neb.

[4] This is a term I have coined. A dialect is usually understood as an inferior language variation. Yet, communication scholar Suzanne Romaine points out: "Dialects . . . have to do with boundaries . . . often, of a social nature, [in which] case we may speak of 'social dialects.' Social dialects say who we are . . . regional dialects, where we come from." Those same boundaries exist not only between social classes but also between generations. Suzanne Romaine, "Language in Society/Society in Language" in *Language in Society: An Introduction to Sociolinguistics* (London: Oxford University Press, 1994) 2.

fifteen-year-old teenager about to get her driver's license who has only known economic and national security until 9/11. An editorial in the St. Louis *The University News* on September 13, 2001, entitled "A Day That Will Live on in Infamy," described this latter generation's new sense of insecurity:

> We didn't witness the bombing of Pearl Harbor . . . hide under desks . . . for Cold War threats [or fight to stay alive] in the jungles of Vietnam. . . . [Instead], we've seen the . . . victory of freedom . . . the Berlin Wall fell to the ground . . . Saddam Hussein [was defeated] . . . communism [collapsed] and democracy [rose] in the former Soviet Union. Our lives have been consumed by neither war nor threats, [but] . . . have been full of . . . expanding capitalism. Monday night, [9/10], we . . . went to sleep—full of naïveté. Tuesday . . . we woke up to a different world. The [attack on the] mighty United States . . . shatter[ed] our fragile innocence . . . our generation grew up.[5]

There must be a homiletic, therefore, that is able to effectively work through the lens of generation in order to engage the Good News with the differing worldviews of the varied generations. That reflects, in fact, the heart of the matter for this book: advocating for preachers to "address issues present in every generation, albeit in different garb and guises."[6] The preacher's challenge then is to be intentionally cognizant of the unique characteristics of each generation assembled to hear the Word at the same time and in the same setting. I argue against the current well intentioned, but misguided practice of having the younger generations leave during the Liturgy of the Word and homily. I also argue against the institutionalization of Teen Life Masses. In attempting to solve one problem, both scenarios create another.

Where does this issue really begin to take focus? In a rapidly changing technological society, generational differences are accelerated and magnified. Technology accelerates change that then acceler-

[5] Editorial, "A Day That Will Live in Infamy," *The University News*, September 13, 2001, 5, as quoted by Dorothy Jonaitis, O.P., *Unmasking Apocalyptic Preaching: Cosmic Drama of Hope*, thesis project, Aquinas Institute of Theology, May 2002, 83.

[6] The Bishops Conference on Priestly Life and Ministry: National Committee of Catholic Bishops, *Fulfilled in Your Hearing: The Homily in the Sunday Assembly* (Washington, D.C.: United States Catholic Conference, 1982) 46.

ates the mobility of generations, actually creating new and distinct generations faster than ever before. As this phenomenon occurs, the boundaries between generations become narrower and less fluid. So a generational shift that once occurred over thirty years now takes place in fifteen and soon will be even less. For instance, in ancient Rome, because people only lived to thirty years of age and social change occurred at a snail's pace, there was really only one generation. By the time the human race progressed through the Renaissance and people began living to age fifty, you had three or more generations. Now in the twenty-first century with change coming so fast we can barely keep up, the number of years between generations has decreased dramatically, leaving us with and on the cusp of six generations.

Studies have been offered concerning how to communicate individually with these generations. However, there is a dearth of information about how to speak collectively to them, which is the more common situation of preachers weekend after weekend. Some argue that the "generational divide" is so pronounced that it prohibits effective preaching to all age groups at the same time. Yet, if preaching is to be relevant and life giving, and be true to its ultimate task of unifying the Christian community, it must find a way to achieve this precise end!

I believe I have found one way to meet the challenge of intergenerational preaching. By studying communication and marketing theory, particularly in a Catholic context, the seismic impact of language and culture in the construction of generational and religious identities becomes readily apparent.

The process I have used also examines what the preacher can learn from the marketer through a qualified use of current market segmentation practices. In the same way marketers learn everything they can about their target audiences to know how to tailor the advertiser's words to address consumer desires, so must preachers know their various audiences to carefully choose words that address spiritual hungers when proclaiming the gospel message.

When preparing a homily, it is standard practice to exegete a text. But what if we exegete generationally those who are going to hear the text? Wouldn't that make a major difference? It is important to clearly note, however, that preachers eventually depart from the goals of marketers because the marketers' ultimate purpose is to keep their segments divided as separate islands unto themselves. Preachers seek similar means but to ultimately achieve the opposite result: bringing their segments together into a unified whole, a community.

Finally, in situating this discussion in a Catholic context, I explore areas of Catholic generational differences, including issues of clear generational agreement and disagreement among the three generational Catholic cohorts: Pre-Vatican II, Vatican II, and Post-Vatican II. Utilizing theologian Joseph Webb's *hub symbol* theory, I examine how the sacramental context of the Catholic tradition forms natural trans-generational hub symbols from which to design a multi-generational homiletic. What do I mean by hub symbol? Webb would say everyone has certain emotionally charged experiences formed generally in the very early years of life upon which they place a value. Those experiences with the greatest intensity of value form the hub of one's symbolic worldview and become central pillars in our lives the way hubs form the center of a bike wheel. So if one entered a room with forty people sitting in it, one would be encountering forty different symbolic universes. Thus, our conversations or interactions through the medium of language are not simply made up of words and grammatical pauses. When we meet and talk, two separate and sacred symbolic universes meet and are in conversation with one another.

My hypothesis was tested through practical application in three intergenerational parish settings. I prepared and preached an actual intergenerational homily by utilizing the specific knowledge of the cultural and Catholic characteristics of each of the five generations discussed in this book and obtained feedback through written and oral evaluation. I did this by taking the theme for that gospel and choosing specific images, metaphors, and linguistic references targeted to draw in each generation, some in a light-hearted way, others through deeper nuances.

At the conclusion of the book, there are practical suggestions on how one can begin the journey or hone the craft of becoming an effective and credible intergenerational preacher.

Why Effective Preaching Is a Priority: The Problem

1

Dwindling weekend Mass attendance (especially among the young), the flight of Catholics to nondenominational *mega-churches* and the consistent sense of boredom among even dutiful Catholics who do regularly attend Eucharist all reflect stagnation within Catholic preaching. Walter Burghardt, S.J., an internationally renowned preacher, does not mince words in his assessment:

> Our homilies are rarely heretical. They fail, fall short, flounder rather because they are stale and flat, vapid and insipid, dreadfully dry and boringly barren. One reason? They are not pregnant with the inexhaustible riches that is Christ; they carry so little substance, so little sap to slake the parched spirit.[1]

In discerning my own experience as a Roman Catholic priest and that of Catholics who have spoken with me over the years, I suggest this results from the following six elements:

1. Lack of exegetical preparation, both scriptural and congregational;
2. Poor and unenthusiastic delivery;
3. Failure to address social issues or catechesis concerning essential beliefs of the faith;
4. Lack of connection with events of daily life;

[1] Walter J. Burghardt, S.J., quoted in Edward Ruane, O.P., "The Spirituality of the Preacher" in *In the Company of Preachers* (Collegeville: The Liturgical Press, 1993) 161.

5. No continuity week to week with the Scriptural message;

6. Lack of cultural or *generational* relevance.

Many Catholic preachers simply do not take the time needed to prepare a good homily. Some will even admit that fact but defend themselves, saying they have little time left over after running the parish plant and program operations. Many note that the heyday of having three to five priests to share pastoral and sacramental duties is over. Others bemoan the fact that the Roman Catholic hierarchy is not at all disposed to the ordination of women or even to allowing them to preach during the celebration of the Eucharist. I suspect that the overriding truth, despite the Second Vatican Council's clear enunciation of preaching as the first responsibility of priests (Decree on the Ministry and Life of Priests), is that other functions simply take precedence over the obligation for good preaching preparation.

John Lennon had a saying: "Life is what happens when we are making other plans." Too often preaching is just "what happens" when priests are busy "doing" other things. In fairness, sometimes that reality is within the control of the priest and sometimes it is not. What is significant for our purposes is that men who came to the church to be priests have too often become harried, preoccupied, overworked CEOs. Placed alongside everything else in their day, preaching just "happens." They enter the pulpit devoid of exegetical insight and of an enthusiastic and relevant Christian vision, much less a perspective sensitive to the multiple generations arrayed before them. "Where there is no vision, the people perish," says Proverbs 29:18. The preaching proverb is: "Where there is no preparation, the preaching perishes!" An intergenerational approach to preaching is one way to retrieve an exciting vision for one's preaching.

While most priests have the benefit of a very solid theological education, their capacity to preach from a biblical base is not evident in the pulpit. Is this due to a *laissez-faire* approach to preaching or more of the above fatigue and lack of prioritization? Scriptural exegesis prior to a homily would make a difference if preachers also took time to *exegete their assembly*. Exegesis is generally understood as the interpretation of the biblical text. An exegesis of one's congregation entails knowing who is there Sunday after Sunday. At the very least, the preacher needs to know the general demographics of race, ethnicity, gender, and age if he/she hopes to speak with any relevance. It also

means knowing, as much as possible, what personal and communal issues are foremost in parishioners' minds and hearts.

Similar, but not identical to how successful marketing strategies depend upon identifying and fulfilling the needs and wants of consumers, successful preachers must discover and address the *spiritual consumers* in their pews each weekend. What are the spiritual needs of the assembled faithful? What are the inner benefits of faith for which they hunger? The qualification to this analogy is that for preachers there is a difference between real needs and mere wants, whereas for marketers, needs and wants are for all practical purposes, synonymous. Like the marketer, the preacher must remember one product rarely addresses the diverse needs and wants of all consumers. The key for both is being attentive to the myriad ways different groups of people receive what preacher and marketer have to offer to meet those needs and wants. As successful marketers adapt their marketing programs to meet the specific needs of their target groups, so must preachers. Insofar as their homiletic approach acknowledges that different groups of people hear, recognize and benefit from the gospel message in different ways, they have learned from marketers the route to effectiveness.

Scripture cannot come alive as a living force if the exegesis of the biblical word is not brought in creative tension with an exegesis of the everyday world of one's parishioners. Just as we exegete a text to discern its historic context, we also need to recognize the human, and in particular the generational, context every Sunday morning. Many preachers simply don't bother to take this extra step because it has never occurred to them or because they don't regard it as essential. This results in a mismatching of what we preach and to whom we are preaching. Preaching is never exercised in a vacuum but in a cultural context, and, as I argue throughout this book, a generational one. When intergenerational sensitivity is appreciated as an integral part of the homiletic communication method, it is then positioned to meet and speak to this multi-generational, cultural context.

In the past, the Roman Catholic Church was known for its catechetical preaching, emphasizing doctrines of faith and not Scripture. On the one hand, current preaching has tended toward the scriptural end of the spectrum. On the other hand, it often lacks even that and is seemingly devoid of Catholic teaching, history, and tradition. Greater catechetical substance that informs faith in the Word of God is needed, but so is substance that is culturally attuned and generationally relevant. As John Roberto, a generational theorist, cautions: "We need to approach faith formation as a missionary, not an entrenched catechist."[2] Preachers are transparent in the pulpit. If they are not enthused about the Word, how can they expect others to be? A dry delivery usually signals a dry preparation and homiletic approach that bears none of the marks of the zeal of a missionary.

What is particularly striking about this situation is that the Scriptures so easily lend themselves to generational dialogue. The story of salvation history is replete with examples of generations of faith from Abraham to Moses to David. Yet, from week to week we don't hear the connection between these stories and the modern stories (e.g., Dietrich Bonhoeffer and Mother Teresa). God is revealed continually through peoples of all times and places, to people of all ages and races. The communion of all reality achieves the vision of communal reconciliation. This includes an intergenerational vision of connectedness.

Does the preceding description constitute a crisis in preaching? The following explores this question from two angles: a recent study and the comments of Catholic and Protestant scholars.

A. How Catholics See the Problem

The sentiments expressed by this writer are supported by the findings of a recent study undertaken by Barbara Reid, O.P., and Leslie Hoppe, O.F.M., two members of the biblical literature and languages department of Catholic Theological Union (CTU).[3] Both Reid and Hoppe teach Scripture at CTU and are concerned about the formation of future preachers. With that interest in mind, they undertook a study to ascertain how preachers utilize Scripture both in their homiletic preparation and Sunday preaching. The impetus for the project was two-fold: (1) The low quality of Catholic preaching they experienced that confirmed the poor public reputation of ordained Roman Catholic preachers, and (2) the prioritization of preaching in the Archdiocese of Chicago's strategic plan.

[2] Comment by generation theorist John Roberto at the May 31–June 1, 2000, Generations of Faith workshop in Omaha, Neb.

[3] Barbara E. Reid, O.P., and Leslie J. Hoppe, O.F.M., *Preaching from the Scriptures: New Directions for Preparing Preachers* (Chicago: Catholic Theological Union, 1998).

The researchers found many concerned about the quality of preaching: bishops, diocesan planning boards, seminary personnel, preachers, and members of congregations. Amid the diverse voices, the concern was uniform: Catholic preachers do not effectively bridge biblical exegesis and cultural context within a liturgical proclamation. Reid and Hoppe suggest that a pedagogical problem exists at the heart of that failure. Perhaps the most startling finding of the study is that merely one-fourth of the preachings evaluated offered any suggestion or hint of exegetical preparation. The irony of this finding is that those participating in the study were educated in modern critical methods of biblical interpretation. These preachers, however, showed scant evidence of that training. The most salient conclusions are summarized in the following chart:

Criteria	**Percent**
Cites the text	96
Rephrases the text	66
Explains cultural realities of the text	16
Leads congregation to identify with the story's characters	73
Engages theological views of the text	21
Aware of text's theological pluralism	12
Shows how text illumines Christian life	81
Shows how text suggests behaviors	90
Shows evidence of sound exegetical preparation	27[4]

Again, Reid and Hoppe point out that the last statistic is cause for alarm because it impacts all of the above statistics. A majority of homilies in the study did not reflect solid biblical interpretation or sound theological reflection.

What can we say about these percentages in light of my argument that there is a need for a new vision of preaching from an intergenerational perspective? Positive elements of the report, those behaviors receiving the highest numbers (*viz.,* cite and rephrase the text, show how texts illuminate Christian life and suggest corresponding behaviors, lead congregations to identify their story within the

[4] Ibid., 2.

story's characters) demonstrate the preachers' desire to make the Scriptures relevant, even if they are not successful in doing so. The desire itself can motivate preachers to apply a different perspective or vision in preparation to achieve this goal.

The discouraging news from the findings is the lowest numbers. These reflect not only poor scriptural exegesis but also an inability to explain the cultural realities or the plurality of theological viewpoints. If preachers are not conscious of pluralism in the text or its cultural context, how can they be aware of cultural and pluralistic realities every Sunday? I submit that the lens for both is the same: lacking a biblical, cultural, and theologically pluralistic engagement with the text translates into the same lack of engagement with the assembly. Exegesis of the text concentrates on the events and situations of past generations of faith, while an exegesis of the congregation focuses on the events and situations of present generations of faith with that same Word. An intergenerational perspective approaches both forms of exegesis contributing mightily toward more effective preaching.

Many prominent Catholics, lay and ordained, whether preachers, pastoral musicians or sociologists, also have voiced concern over the current state of preaching in the church. In *Preaching the Just Word* Burghardt summarizes his feelings: "Catholic preaching, for all its upsurge since the Second Vatican Council (1962–1965), is not our most successful ministry."[5] He unhappily affirms a famous comment by Dennis O'Brien, president of the University of Rochester, that Monday morning commuters would describe church the previous day as "Saturday Night Live, Sunday Morning Deadly."[6]

While the critique is painfully accurate, the reasons for unsuccessful preaching are more nuanced than inadvertantly speaking heretical statements. The "sap" that Burghardt's "parched spirits" are looking for and what O'Brien's weary commuters attest to be missing is the relevance of the Word to the concrete, lived experience of their everyday lives. Preachers do not know their congregants' issues. Therefore, they lack passion and lose the fire gained from intergenerational sensitivity and engagement. Tom Booth, director of music for the National Life Teen Program, puts the issue bluntly:

[5] Walter J. Burghardt, S.J., *Preaching the Just Word* (New Haven: Yale University Press, 1996) ix.

[6] Ibid., ix.

> Why do our homilists tend to be so boring? Why do we approach the Gospel of Jesus Christ as if it were something to be spoken in a drone void of emotion, as though it were not something to be passionate about? I remember "surviving" a liturgy once.[7]

Booth's experience is unfortunately not uncommon. That priests lack passion for their ministry of preaching and presiding is an all too familiar complaint from the pews. Sometimes this is most apparent when people compliment the presider after Mass saying: "Thank you, Father, that was such a 'spiritual' Mass." Such a comment has always struck me as a redundancy! The Sunday celebration should be spiritual by nature. Yet that is not people's experience at the adult as well as the teenage level. Strikingly enough, while older adults are the more faithful and consistent churchgoers, this lack of spirit is an intergenerational experience. A prominent lay Catholic liturgist David Haas bemoans this very problem: young people *and* adults are bored at Mass, seeing little connection between the liturgical event and the circumstances and events of their everyday lives.

These rumblings have been heard and acknowledged by the Roman Catholic Church, which shares some of their own related concerns:

> One of the reasons our preaching is less effective than it could be is that we have not taken seriously enough the *lectio continua* principle of our lectionary. We preach each Sunday homily as if it had no connection with what preceded or will follow.[8]

Boredom in the pews from bad preaching results in a severe lack of connection. There is no connection because the preacher is not relating to the parishioners about their life experiences. There is no connection because there is no appreciation for those living in a generationally historic moment carrying all the baggage and opportunities of their generation's issues with faith and religion. We continually dance around this essential issue. We preach each Sunday as if the lives, the joys and struggles, of those assembled were no different week to week and no different generationally. Just as we don't follow the *lectio continua* principle of the Lectionary, we don't comprehend or follow the *generatio continua* motif of the biblical story.

[7] Tom Booth, "Life Teen: 'A Mass That Became a Youth Ministry Movement,'" *Pastoral Music* 24, no. 5 (June–July 2000) 22.

[8] *Fulfilled in Your Hearing,* 30.

There is pessimism from all levels of the Church that preaching is ineffectual. How do we retrieve the power of preaching that has nurtured and sustained the growth of the Church throughout the ages? Catholic priest and sociologist Andrew Greeley agrees with the mournful chorus about poor preaching. He suggests an interesting antidote: renew preaching by preaching! This renewed preaching would be:

- Parish-centered
- Focused on the core beliefs of Christianity
- Excellent (less than one out of five American Catholics think that the homilies they hear are excellent).[9]

This kind of preaching, Greeley states, would revivify Catholicism.

Carrying Greeley's thinking a step further, I offer this thought: More effective than parish-centered preaching, which is focused on the core beliefs of Catholic Christianity, would be *generation-centered* preaching focused on relating each age group's religious experience and spiritual outlook to the essential beliefs of Christianity. Preaching, which has as its precision and depth an intergenerational foundation, makes for truly excellent parish preaching!

B. How Protestants See the Problem

While this book's primary focus is on the impoverished situation of Catholic preaching, Protestants' concerns about their own preaching are both instructive and transferable. Lenora Tubbs Tisdale, assistant professor of preaching and worship at Princeton University, argues for a more contextual approach to preaching. She advocates a competent exegesis of one's congregation as a normative part of sermon preparation. Tisdale's concern emanates from an overemphasis on the psychological needs hearers bring as well as human experience. She points out the danger of the preaching event being reduced to simply healing people psychologically, absenting itself from the Gospel's ethical and social challenges.

[9] Andrew Greeley quoted in Richard Hart, O.F.M. Cap., *Preaching: The Secret to Parish Revival* (Mystic, Conn.: Twenty-Third Publications/Bayard, 2000) 1.

Tisdale also cites the most common errors of Protestant seminary preaching courses with a critique that is also applicable to Catholic seminary curricula:

- They [students and pastors] prepare generic sermons for generic humanity that never becomes truly enfleshed in the real-life situations of particular congregations
- They paint overly simplistic pictures of their hearers in preaching, attributing to them attitudes, beliefs, or values that they do not actually hold
- They project onto congregations—unconsciously and unintentionally—their own issues and concerns.[10]

Tisdale's passionate argument for an exegesis of the preacher's congregation as part of the homiletic process is on the money. After all, preachers preach first to themselves. If the inadequacies listed above are to be remedied, she proposes a clear solution: the preacher must identify the different subcultures that exist within the corporate community of our Sunday assemblies. Tisdale believes that effective preachers are conscious of the multi-faceted, *multi-agendaed* subgroups that exist alongside one another in an assembly. This book's argument is that generation is one of Tisdale's subcultures and should be a conscious concern of the preacher. Preachers who cannot name generational characteristics of their own will fail in identifying attitudes, beliefs and values that comprise the many age groups to whom they preach. This renders the preacher much less effective or engaging in the pulpit.

A consistent and constant voice for wedding culture and preaching is Henry Mitchell. Primarily known for his writing on black preaching, Mitchell identifies the ineffectiveness of white, American preachers with their inability to speak to their congregations in culturally relevant ways. Instead, they speak to the folk idiom of America's majority. His eloquent words can be equally applied to the case for intergenerational sensitivity:

> Whether in the Black ghetto, the affluent suburb, or the uttermost parts of the earth, the deepest and most meaningful cultural

[10] Lenora Tubbs Tisdale, *Preaching as Local Theology and Folk Art* (Minneapolis: Fortress Press, 1997) 19.

> *[including generational]* heritage of persons must be identified, respected and built upon. . . . Preaching that makes meaningful impact on lives has to reach persons at gut level, and it is at this level of communally stored wisdom and cultural affinity that such access to living souls is gained.[11]

A relevant, complementary observation on Mitchell's assertion is David Buttrick's contention that many of us no longer find the words of another credible. He claims that we are, in fact, tired of words and are encountering in today's society a malaise of sorts. In his seminal work *Homiletic*, Buttrick reflects:

> Nothing is more peculiar than the church's loss of confidence in language. [Is not] the church . . . built on the testimony of apostles, martyrs and saints? Yet, today we stammer. About the only people left who believe in the power of words are poets and revolutionaries. We, who are a people of the Word, are wordless.[12]

Buttrick draws attention to the impact of not only our words today but those of countless generations before us. An intergenerational preacher recognizes the power of the spoken word and how its critical import varies from generation to generation. Recalling Walter Burghardt's assessment, when preachers are not sensitive to the assembled age groups and their different vocabularies or special meanings for ordinary words, they fall flat. Burghardt's thesis is too often proven true.

From a diversity of voices, both Protestant and Catholic, the concern for the situation of Christian preaching is palpable! Increasingly, experts and practitioners in the field of homiletics are acknowledging a crisis, particularly in Catholic preaching. Whether due solely and specifically to the myriad reasons cited above, it is incumbent upon church ministers, lay and ordained, to ascertain the *why* of the crisis and offer solutions. It should now be readily apparent that it is my view that intergenerational sensitivity at both the exegetical and homiletic level would help alleviate this crisis. Having established what ails current preaching, let us look more closely at the historically Catholic approach to "the homily." Perhaps we can see how inter-

[11] Henry H. Mitchell, quoted in Tisdale, 21 [italics mine].

[12] David Buttrick, *Homiletic: Moves and Structures* (Philadelphia: Fortress Press, 1987) 5–6.

generational sensitivity, while not a once-and-for-all panacea, might offer a new way to address the problem thereby yielding new life for preaching.

The Genesis of the Catholic Homily 2

The term "homily" does not appear frequently in the early Church. Interestingly enough, it is the word *keryssein,* ("to proclaim"), not *homileo,* that has the more common usage in the New Testament. The distinction between the two is that the former refers to preaching to unbelievers and the latter to those already considered part of the faithful. Reflections on the Scriptures after their proclamation were part of the established order in Jewish synagogues at the time of Jesus. Nevertheless, they were not considered homilies in the way we define that term today, namely as "the exposition of a text of Scripture which takes place in and as part of a liturgical celebration."[1] What is important is that some form of instruction followed the Scripture readings, and it is from this scriptural base of our Jewish ancestors that we draw our idea for the homily today. In *Fulfilled in Your Hearing: The Homily in the Sunday Assembly,* the American bishops underscore this central theme. The homily is:

> a scriptural interpretation of human existence which enables a community to recognize God's active presence, to respond to that presence in faith through liturgical word and gesture, and beyond the liturgical assembly, through a life lived in conformity with the Gospel.[2]

The bishops coin a key phrase that resonates throughout the above citation: Scriptural interpretation of human existence—"which is experientially relevant to all." The CTU study cited earlier summarizes

[1] *Fulfilled in Your Hearing,* 46.
[2] Ibid., 29.

that most people's experience Sunday after Sunday is precisely the opposite. Preachers not only do not appear to grasp the substance of the text upon which they are preaching, but demonstrate no clear propensity to make the Scripture relevant to the daily experience of those assembled. We have seen from the other categories and their corresponding numbers (90 percent of preachers' homilies show an intent to illumine Christian life; 81 percent demonstrate how the scriptural text suggests [Christian] behaviors) that the problem lies not so much in a complete lack of desire to make this connection but perhaps, the best means to achieve this end. I argue that a generationally nuanced preaching offers a highly effective and creative means.

How do preachers move from exegesis to effectively interpreting the Scriptures through the lived experience of their assembly? What is the lens one uses with which to prepare and proclaim the Word? While no one hermeneutic is superior to another, one promising cultural hermeneutical lens is consistently overlooked, that of generation. I suspect that Catholic preachers are not in the habit of recognizing the arguably five or six generations (i.e., demographic groups) that regularly comprise their Sunday assembly. I also suspect that those who do recognize generational differences often dismiss their importance, subscribing to the fatal and misguided rule of thumb: preach broadly to the middle of the congregation and hope it will land on as many as possible! That faulty thinking is perpetuated by the unsound presumption that one can only preach to one generation at a time. Hence, there is a tendency to divide a congregation: children to their Sunday morning catechesis and teenagers to special teen Masses. This is essentially self-defeating, especially for teens, who seldom are successfully integrated into the larger congregation.

In an article on this topic, David Haas expresses succinctly the dangers of liturgical separation:

> Liturgy is an activity that proclaims unity: it is a call to come out from our isolation, a call to true communion. Separate liturgies for separate groupings of people goes against all that we believe we are called to be as the Body of Christ. Separate worship according to age unintentionally fosters the breakdown of family and community.[3]

[3] David Haas, "We Don't Need Vibrant Worship 'with Youth'; We Need Vibrant Worship, Period," *Pastoral Music* 24, no. 5 (June–July 2000) 39.

It is the belief of other liturgical theologians that Haas's approach is more effective for long-term intergenerational faith formation. I agree with them. Effective preaching recognizes and embraces the generational composition of faith communities that gather each Sunday for the Word and Eucharist. At least one of the solutions for the poor reputation of current Catholic preaching is embracing the connection of generations as a powerful avenue to renew and reenergize this central and critical moment of the Sunday liturgical celebration. In his *Preaching: The Secret to Parish Revival,* Richard Hart, O.F.M., highlights the need for this generational perspective:

> Senior citizens, baby boomers, generation x-ers, and teenagers each have different outlooks on life. What are these outlooks, and how does a preacher address them effectively, especially when the assembly ranges in age from eight to eighty.[4]

Table 1, which draws from the work of generation theorists John Roberto and Ronald Allen, offers a general compilation of the dominant values and characteristics of five current generations.[5]

Roberto and Allen's work, as well as other recent articles and studies, offer intriguing insights about the religious perspectives of our current generations. What can we glean from these assessments? What can preachers keep in mind about each generation as they develop a homily?

Generally, Generation-Xers have shown that authentic witness and credibility is consistently and strongly desired. This is all the more intriguing when one notes that the defining reality of the generation preceding the Xers is the unequivocal rejection of structure. The Baby Boomers threw off the shackles of structure and authority. Thus, the generation following the Boomers wants to retrieve structure and authority, not as a paralyzing, top-down phenomenon but as liberation from the social and religious chaos that marks its contemporary experience. On the other hand, the generation preceding the Boomers, the Silent Generation, appears to be in tandem with the Xers in longing for a return to authority and structure. But an important clarification is that the Silent Generation was comfortable with external authority. Xers have shifted the seat of authority from external to internal.

[4] Hart, 7.

[5] Allen, 369–400, and Roberto, 12–15.

Let us compare these outlooks against the shoot for the broad middle approach and the cookie-cutter mentality favored by some preachers. Examples from the automobile industry might be instructive. The General Motors Corporation, founded in 1920, was built on the premise that by appealing to five different consumer groups under a natural hierarchy of socio-economically distinct and status-conscious divisions such as Chevrolet, Pontiac, and Oldsmobile, it would be successful. That assumption turned out to be accurate and, for some sixty years, GM was tremendously successful. That success dramatically stalled when those distinctions that undergirded their original philosophy became blurred.

The gradual *generisizing* of previously distinct products subsequently demonstrated GM management's failure to fully acknowledge the differences within the varied consumer groups.[6] In fact, as of this writing, GM has announced the cessation of the 103-year-Oldsmobile line because it "came to be seen as dowdy."[7] Dealers were upset that GM had abandoned older buyers in the last five years in order to court younger, better educated customers. Just as in the case of GM, a shoot for the broad middle mentality does not make for successful preaching! Like the five different consumer groups, five varied generations in the same congregation must be drawn individually by acknowledging and respecting their unique characteristics.

That's all the more true for the one-size-fits-all cookie-cutter approach of Henry Ford's mass-marketed Model T, recalled in his legendary quote: "They can have any color they want as long as it's black." It is this one-size fits all mentality and an approach that blurs very real differences between distinct groups of people that have significantly contributed to the crisis in preaching. "The proverbial sermon 'barrel' is helpful only as far as the universals of human experience will carry it."[8] The position of this writer is that one major reason for this homiletic poverty is the continuous blurring of generational differences and needs in the Sunday assembly. The CTU study supports this thesis. It showed not only a surprising lack of exegetical preparation among Catholic preachers but also a lack of relevant explanation of cultural realities and theological pluralism. These would

[6] William L. Wilkie, "Market Segmentation" in *Consumer Behavior*, 3rd ed. (New York: John Wiley & Sons, 1994) 84.

[7] *The New York Times*, Business/Finance Section (December 13, 2000).

[8] Tisdale, 41.

Table 1: Generations' Values and Characteristics

Builders (1901–1924) *"The Institutional Generation"*	Dedication/sacrifice Respect for authority Hard work Conformity Law and order Security/stability	Committed to church/ community Linear, uncritical outlook Traditional beliefs/practices Minister out of responsibility Loyal/moral obligation to God "Construct a society"
Silent (1925–1942) *"Bridge Builders"*	Patience Adherence to rules Duty before pleasure Delayed reward Honor	Commit to justice/public good Conversation/dialogue People first concern Flexibility/reconciliation Bureaucratic/ "Keep society together"
Baby Boomers (1943–1961/64) *"Visionaries and Seekers"*	Optimism Team Orientation/pluralistic Propensity toward confrontation Immediate gratification Personal choice/growth	Seek purpose Spiritual, not religious Family-oriented/community Democratic, not authoritarian "Justify, purify, sanctify society"
Generation X (1961/64–1981) *"A Relational Generation"*	Institutional Disillusionment Technoliteracy Self-reliant, but relational Informal/pragmatic/tolerant Personal experience/relativistic	Shaped by popular culture Interactive/nonlinear/critical Suspicious of "absolutes" Relationship vs. accomplishment "Make *self* right, then society"
Millennial (1981–present) *"Young Navigators"*	Optimism Confidence/sociability Morality/"street-smarts" Civic duty/achievement Diversity	Open to explore, investigate Being connected Multi-media savvy/imaginal Spirituality, communally hungry Service/"Do my part socially"

be more forthcoming if an exegesis of the assembly's generational makeup were a consistent part of the homiletic process.

My overall critique is that current preaching suffers from three perennial flaws:

1. Lack of exegetical preparation, or;
2. Exegetical preparation that is too focused (i.e., appealing to only one generation [presumably older] or to the generation of the preacher himself) or;
3. Exegetical preparation that is unfocused (i.e., targeted to "everyone in general," but "no one in particular").

Like GM marketing executives, preachers need to recognize the death knell of this cookie-cutter approach in preaching and regroup with substantive and appealing homiletic strategies. Homiletic strategies could draw significant value and insight from contemporary market segmentation practices and the strategies underlying their approach. The regrouping proposed would juxtapose the homiletic goals with the imagination of the preacher, trying to reach multiple generations of Sunday worshipers in the same way the marketer tries to reach multiple generations of consumers. This involves new homiletic communication methods and content styles that take into account generations that are:

- Visual, nonlinear and imaginal learners (Generation X and Millennial: 1961/64–1981)
- Traditional, linear and propositional learners (Builders & Silent Generations: 1901–1946)

What would the broad and practical outline of that juxtaposition look like? Before this question can be answered, we need a basic understanding of the dynamics of language and culture and their role in the construction of generational self-understanding. To that subject, we now turn.

3 Intergenerational Preaching as a Sacred Dance between Culture, Language, and Meaning

"The power of verse is derived from an indefinable harmony between what it [the verse] *says* and what it *is*. Indefinable is essential to the definition."[1] What Paul Valery suggests about poetry is also an accurate descriptor of the power of language. It is a powerful but limited medium always open to interpretation. Contrary to prevailing assumptions, there is no one imaginary linguistic center. This is especially true when viewed through generational lens.

Witness the following interaction between the pastor of a local campus ministry site and myself during an introductory visit:

AW 1: "Thank you for making the time to see me with your busy schedule."

P 1: "Hey, it's just awesome that we could connect."

AW 2: "Well, I'm glad we could get together. I'm interested in seeing where I can help out."

P 2: "That's great, really awesome! What's your 100 percent for 'Wash U'?"

AW 3: "Ah, excuse me?"

P 3: "Your 100 percent?"

AW 4: "Well, I . . . You know Gary, I really have no clue what you are asking me."

[1] Paul Valery quoted in *How to Read a Poem* by Edward Hirsch (New York: Harcourt Brace, 1999) xi.

P 4: (Chuckle) "Oh, I'm sorry, that's just how we talk around here. When we have our meetings, you know, the kids and I, we go around the table and tell each other what our 100 percent is for the project or event, what our ideal hope or turnout would be for that project. So Andrew Carl, what would be for you the ideal situation or outcome for your working here at Wash U?"

Because of his choice of language, this scenario demonstrates my initial, complete lack of comprehension of the pastor's inquiry. It was all the more interesting considering that the writer is closer in age to the youth served in the campus ministry than the pastor. Furthermore, the pastor drew from a *generational dictionary* outside his own generation. Clearly his nine years working with youth has formed his choice of vocabulary and his presumption that it is universally understood.

In this book, the locus for culture is generation and the exchange above illustrates its focus. How is the cultural community of age created by language? How does our use of language reflect the different generations? In short, how do language and the arguably five or six current generations influence one another? Addressing these questions is critical if a preacher is to know how to effectively craft a homily so that preaching has the best opportunity to be effectively heard by *all* the generations represented in the assembly.

How do preachers speak in a language that tells their listeners that they know, respect and will speak competently and effectively to each generation? Preachers must have a fundamental understanding of the significant effect culture, language and communication have in the construction of generations. Protestant theologian Ronald Allen states, "Each generation finds certain qualities of communication appealing, and other qualities less so. These qualities are related to the larger life journeys of each generation."[2]

Intergenerational preaching is a sacred dance. The challenge of communicating through culture, language and meaning can be likened to learning the necessary steps to engage in that dance respectfully and competently. These pages will demonstrate not only what such a capacity looks like but also the grace that emanates from the dance when it is achieved!

[2] Allen, 370.

A. The Dance of Culture

A fundamental understanding of culture is essential to gleaning those qualities of each generation alluded to by Allen above. What is culture and how does it relate to each generation's worldview?[3] Richard Porter and Larry Samover define culture as:

> the deposit of knowledge, experience, beliefs, values, attitudes, meanings, hierarchies, religion, notions of time, spatial relations, concepts of the universe and material objects and possessions acquired by a group of people in the course of generations through individual and group striving.[4]

This deposit can be divided into three categories: artifacts, concepts and behaviors. *Artifacts* relate to the possessions of a culture, the products by which they define themselves such as tie-dye shirts, music, scooters, Stetson hats, WWJD[5] wristbands, body piercing or tattoos. *Concepts* comprise the beliefs, values or attitudes of our cultural frameworks. These concepts revolve around issues of meaning relating to how we approach God, the cosmos, humanity, morality and our life's work. *Behaviors* refer to how we practically live out these concepts.[6]

This breakdown is enormously relevant to generations. It defines how each age group comes to instinctively know itself and *selectively* identify itself.[7] It provides *ethnocentric* lenses through which they eventually see not only the world but also judge their and everyone else's place in the world.[8] A whole cultural worldview is formed and shaped

[3] I agree with Porter and Samovar's definition of worldview as dealing "with a culture's orientation toward such philosophical issues as God, humanity, nature, the universe, and others concerned with the concept of being. . . . Our world view helps us locate our place and rank in the universe." Richard E. Porter and Larry A. Samovar, "An Introduction to Intercultural Communication," *Intercultural Communication* (Belmont, Calif.: Wadsworth, 1997) 17.

[4] Ibid., 12.

[5] WWJD wristbands are popular cultural artifacts among young age groups and they mean: *What Would Jesus Do?* They have received public acceptance as cool artifacts even though they publicly designate someone as "religiously-minded."

[6] Porter and Samovar, 13.

[7] Ibid., 14–15. By *selectivity*, our authors mean the limited choice of behavior patterns that every culture chooses from the infinite patterns of human experience.

[8] Ibid., 15. Ethnocentricism is defined by Felix M. Keesing as a "universal tendency for any people to put its own culture and society in a central position of priority and worth."

through the prism of each generation's familial, social, political and religious experiences. Culture therefore is not a stagnant, once-and-for-all-time established reality, but an ongoing, constantly changing dynamic that is both learned and transmittable. The cataclysmic social and political shift of the 1960s offers clear testimony to the truth of this continuing phenomenon. Veteran pollster Daniel Yankelovich calls this period of time "the Consciousness Revolution."[9]

Yankelovich claims that this revolution dramatically changed how Americans saw themselves and the milieu in which they lived. These shifts in perception occurred along generational lines. That era of the Kennedy and King assassinations, the Vietnam War and the Kent State shooting, wrapped up by the Watergate scandal, left each generation to sort out its own trauma. World War I great-grandparents found this a time of angry humiliation and fierce division. Our depression-era grandparents experienced this period as one of personal passages wherein their lives became more turbulent and adventuresome. For our parents, it was a positive, life-giving historical moment that they found personally freeing. For Generation X-ers, that time can only be approached retrospectively from a viewpoint of sociological and political curiosity. A pervading sense exists within this age group that X-ers missed a significant turning point in the political and social calculus of our country's cultural history.[10]

While experienced differently by each age group, these events become a "communal constellation of cultural referents"[11] shared in varying degrees by each generation. The actual memories, historical documenting or later retelling of these events, become fodder for the cultural mill. They represent the "stuff" of the deposit that Porter and Samovar assert are the acquired possessions "in the course of our generational and individual striving."[12]

Each generation therefore is both the recipient and benefactor of a multifaceted cultural deposit wherein one cultural event systematically impacts and touches others. Economist Friedrich Hayek, in a reflection on religion and tradition, puts it succinctly:

[9] Daniel Yankelovich quoted in *The Fourth Turning: An American Prophecy* by William Strauss and Neil Howe (New York: Broadway Books, 1997) 175.

[10] Ibid., 175.

[11] Tom Beaudoin, *Virtual Faith* (San Francisco: Jossey-Bass, 1998) 22.

[12] Ibid., 22.

> Traditions encode the accumulated wisdom of earlier generations in a way that no single generation, however sophisticated, could discover for itself; and it is through learning those traditions and passing them on to our children that we avoid costly mistakes.[13]

Lest we think this a benign but antiquated ideal, an article in *The New York Times* underscores Hayek's point. Speaking about our nation's current culture, columnist Todd Putnam maintains that the 70-plus million young people in our country today look more than ever to their parents as role models.[14] He advises adults concerned with contemporary cultural influences to look not first to Hollywood but within the walls of their own homes. Culture, like charity, begins at home! Equipped with a more solid understanding of culture, we now turn to its relationship with language.

B. The Dance of Language

In her *Speaking Culturally,* Fern Johnson asserts that we live in a "society of increasing linguistic complexity" that at the very least requires "cultural-mindedness."[15] She advocates a language-centered perspective on culture that recognizes the unique role language plays in systematically generating and solidifying meaning in multi-cultural discourse. This discourse, understood as participating social and communications networks, emanates from both native and developed speech communities. Identity is a product of such speech communities, for linguistic perceptions, attitudes, and stereotypes are formed in them. They serve as the base from which language patterns express the beliefs and self-understanding of a particular community.

Generation is one way in which these patterns are culturally determined. The variations we witness in these generational language

[13] Friedrich Hayek quoted in "Markets and Morals" by Jonathan Sacks in *First Things,* no. 105 (August/September 2000) 23.

[14] Todd Putnam, "Behind the Wheel and Driving the Nation's Culture" in *The New York Times: Week In Review Section* (November 2000) 6.

[15] Fern Johnson, *Speaking Culturally: Language Diversity in the United States* (London: Sage Publications, 2000) 3. On p. 5, Johnson defines cultural-mindedness as "the ability to understand that cultural systems play a major role in communicative conduct and symbolic interpretation."

patterns illustrate how language acts as a "social semiotic"[16] within generations. Just as there are language variations popularly labeled as "rap," "black speech," or "gayspeak," one could make a case for "GenX-speak," a unique lexicon of words and expressions attributable to that generation.[17]

Catholic theologian Tom Beaudoin asserts that "the Church is made up of not only sexes, genders, ethnic groups, races and classes; it is also made up of generations."[18] What is the current religious culture to which the intergenerational homilist must preach? Robert Nash offers a brief, but nonetheless, alarmed description:

> With the coming of postmodernity, a new spiritual reality has dawned. We live in an age of easy belief. Churches are surrounded by a culture that is radically pluralistic, highly spiritual, anti-dogmatic, and nonrational. In such a climate, there must be a re-birth of Christian spirituality. A new kind of Christianity must emerge that is exciting, unapologetic, confident, resourceful, and courageous.[19]

For that vision to be recognized, greater attention must be paid to the intersection between language and culture. Johnson's language-centered perspective on culture offers a valuable avenue by which to explore that relationship. She suggests six principles upon which the perspective is rooted:

1. All communication, whether verbal or nonverbal, occurs within cultural frameworks.
2. Individuals possess tacit knowledge of the cultural systems through which they communicate.
3. Groups that have been dominated, subjugated, marginalized, made the object of prejudice and bigotry, discriminated against, or otherwise held in relatively powerless positions possess more explicit awareness of the components of their own and other cultural systems.

[16] Ibid., 29. Johnson is drawing upon M.A.K. Halliday's argument for language as "the centralizing process for the establishment of systemic social meanings."

[17] Most scholars place Generation Xers as those born between 1961/64 and 1981.

[18] Tom Beaudoin, "Beginning Afresh: Gen-X Catholics," *America* 179, no. 16 (1998) 13.

[19] Robert Nash quoted in Roberto, 1.

4. In multicultural societies the ideology of dominant cultural groups produces patterns of cultural abstractions, cultural artifacts, and cultural language practices that displace, silence or marginalize other cultural groups.
5. Culture and its discourse are both passed from one generation to another and constantly revised and changed.
6. In multicultural societies, cultures influence one another, which includes the interinfluence of discourse systems.[20]

These principles are readily applicable to this project as the cultural system of age can be a significant characteristic of these cultural frameworks. I argue, in fact, for just such an expanded view that includes generation.

One's generation impacts how one interacts and how one symbolically understands and interprets communication. The different generations exist as separate speech communities in which language is spoken, understood and deemed meaningful through the agreement of the shared human aggregate of generation. This forms an unspoken understanding of how someone from a particular generation acts and speaks.

In light of the above facts, preachers need to be *generation-minded,* seeking to grasp the interest of a variety of generations at one time. The punch line here is that people listen, speak and act from their generational identities. The preacher can normally discern a person's generation through language. If the language of preachers is so incongruent with the perceptible generations in the congregation, they must seek to understand them from a generational perspective. Recall how my conversation with the pastor described at the beginning of this chapter demonstrated the length to which language can become skewed.[21] What the pastor did can be likened to intergenerational *code-switching.*[22]

In communication theory, code-switching is generally understood as switching back and forth between language styles during a conversation. Scholars such as Johnson, Suzanne Romaine, and Carol Myers

[20] Johnson, 63–67.

[21] This writer did not understand the pastor's use of code language for Generation X *(What's your 100% . . . ?).*

[22] Johnson, 65.

Scotton have explored this practice extensively. Code-switching occurs within particular cultural situations or when different languages are represented.[23] Within a familiar and typical bilingual exchange, no single motivation can be ascribed for code-switching, according to Scotton.[24]

It is my contention that code-switching occurs between different generations of the same language. Its appeal rests in several clear benefits: (1) it enlarges an otherwise limited vocabulary in a particular cultural context, (2) it signals a change from formal to informal discourse, and (3) it "announces specific identities, creates certain meanings and facilitates particular interpersonal role relationships."[25]

The latter function is the most relevant for the concerns of this book because a practice understood and discussed as a bilingual phenomenon can easily be applied to intergenerational dialogue. In this context, code-switching is a "style of language use" whose critical characteristic is not linguistic, but functional.[26] Intergenerational communication such as that with the pastor is an attempt to signal to the other: "I know and can relate to your world." Intergenerational interactions that utilize intentional language variations can make the opposite point: "I have a separate identity."

On the one hand, a particular usage simply reinforces an identification of where and to whom one belongs. On the other hand, usage can clearly delineate "who is in and who is out." Usage could be either positive or negative, depending on motivation, or even neutral, according to Romaine: ". . . code-switching often serves as a strategy of neutrality or as a means to explore which code is most appropriate and acceptable in a particular situation."[27] That motivation varies and could reflect a desire to reinforce solidarity or create distance. Social-linguistics expert J. P. Gee says these are examples of "the exclusion principle," a major operating principle in understanding the meaning behind the language we use ". . . my use of a given word in

[23] This writer has had considerable experience interacting within a community of native English and native Spanish speakers who are somewhat bilingual.

[24] Carol Myers Scotton, "The Negotiation of Identities in Conversation: A Theory of Markedness and Code Choice" in *International Journal of Social Language* (vol. 44, 1983) 122.

[25] Johnson, 185.

[26] Ibid., 187.

[27] Suzanne Romaine, "Language Choice, " in *Language in Society: An Introduction to Sociolinguistics* (London: Oxford Press, 1994) 61.

a given situation is intended to exclude or not exclude. . . . Meaning is always (in part) a matter of intended exclusions and inclusions (contrasts & lack of contrasts) within an assumed semantic field."[28] In either case, code-switching as its own brand of language variation serves as a "badge of community membership."[29] Indeed, in same-generational discourse among one's peers, code-switching can positively reinforce solidarity and mutual social/cultural identity.

A fascinating example of this phenomenon is offered by bell hooks. She recounts the story of black African slaves brought to the "New World" who transformed the English language into their own unique speech patterns. "Enslaved black people took broken bits of English and made of them a counter-language."[30] Just as language can be used negatively as a weapon of oppression, it can also be used positively as a means of rebellion against oppression!

If not approached carefully, however, the preaching that employs generational code-switching risks being perceived as inauthentic and manipulative. Skillfully employed, it offers rich opportunities to connect and resonate with multiple generations at the same time. The standard axiom for anyone involved in cultural code-switching applies as well to the intergenerational preacher: "It requires at least some degree of explicit knowledge about the [generations] from which one is shifting and the [generations] to which one is shifting."[31]

In the meeting with the pastor described above, there was the assumption that since I was willing to work with a particular age group I would understand their current *generational dialect.* A dialect is commonly understood as an unsophisticated form of language usage. But as Suzanne Romaine points out, we may also speak of social dialects along with the concept of *register*:

> Dialects or dialectology has to do with boundaries. Boundaries are, however, often of a social nature, i.e. between different social class groups. In this case, we may speak of "social dialects." Social dialects say who we are, and regional dialects where we come from. . . . While regional dialects reveal where we come from

[28] J. P. Gee, *Social Linguistics and Literacies: Ideology in Discourses* (London: The Falmer Press, 1990) 80.

[29] Johnson, 184.

[30] bell hooks, *Teaching to Transgress Education as the Practice of Freedom* (London: Rautledge, 1994) 170.

[31] Ibid., 65. The original quote used "cultures" instead of generations.

> and social dialects what our status is, register gives us a clue about what we are doing.[32]

Thus, language is not only a marker of cultural identity but can also be an indication of generational identity. It forms, creates and transmits the major meaning system of a generation's self-understanding and identity. Preachers have the challenge of negotiating the borders of each age group's identity. "Vocabulary differences—either a special vocabulary or special meanings for ordinary words—are most important in distinguishing different register."[33]

Homilists need to communicate to different generations that they "can understand you without being one of you." The ability known in linguistic studies as *passing*[34] achieves this goal. Applied to the homiletic strategy of intergenerational preaching, passing refers to preacher's conscious shifts in language use in order to capture the attention of a particular generation in the assembly. This is practically accomplished when preachers succeed in presenting themselves in language *as one of you*. Passing is not just a linguistic reality but a strategic tactic as well. It serves as a strategy for identity when preachers present themselves as members of the group with whom they wish to interact and whose group privileges they wish to avail themselves or, sometimes, to usurp. Common examples of this in today's society are light-skin African Americans passing as white persons among Caucasians, gays passing as straights, men passing as women or the reverse as portrayed in the Oscar-award-winning movie *Boys Don't Cry.*[35]

People can also try to "pass" intergenerationally. Putnam writes about this growing social phenomenon: "Baby boomers are loathe to cede center stage to the coming generations—along with the status that comes from hipness and desirability. So adults have begun sedulously aping teens."[36] In fact, this is becoming so common that it has spawned a new term: *generational blurring.* Irma Zandl, a Manhattan marketing expert, explains:

[32] Romaine, "Language in Society/Society in Language," 2, 20.

[33] Ibid., 20.

[34] Johnson, 42

[35] *Boys Don't Cry* won Best Actress Award for the lead character's portrayal of a lesbian from a small town who, for a time, successfully "passes" for a boy.

[36] Putnam, 1.

> There used to be a certain set of behaviors and ways of dress that if you were an adult you left behind. But as society has become more casual, those rules are really blurred. There isn't that much distinction between how teenagers and adults dress; they're all wearing khakis and jeans and sneakers.[37]

Whether through language use or cultural symbols such as clothes, attempts to "pass" are about repositioning one's identity within a particular setting to receive highly sought after benefits. Homilists, however, can employ this same tactic for the important goal of attracting and maintaining their congregation's attention.

A phrase from one of my recent homilies crafted solely to draw in Generation Xers is linguistically illustrative of this point: "There is a preoccupation in our culture for trying to top every thrill, taste every experience life offers and to have it all right now—we want to keep it coming '24/7/365!'"[38] In using a common mantra of Generation X, I was "passing" as one of them. Accomplished effectively and sincerely, they understood not only the content of my message but its symbolic import: "You can relate to our world."

The homiletic strategy employed in this scenario is also an example of generational code-switching. In this particular instance, select code words (24/7/365) were used to signal a switch away from Baby Boomers and Silent Generation Sunday worshipers to speak specifically to Generation Xers.[39] In shifting to them, I demonstrated an explicit knowledge of their age group's specific identity, choosing conscious language to capture their attention even as I signaled familiarity with the Silent and Baby Boomers Generations from whom I was shifting. What preachers need to do consciously in the pulpit to relate to multiple generations mirrors what all of us already do unconsciously in relating to multiple cultures.

> Each group may have its own norms, values, language as well as ways of speaking, but in order to understand each other and work together people tend to mutually adapt themselves, more or less,

[37] Ibid., 1.

[38] "24/7/365" is a Generation X colloquialism referring to the 24 hours of a day, the 7 days of a week, and the 365 days of the year. Its figurative meaning is: "nonstop or endless."

[39] Previous to the 24/7/365 phrase, I quoted Federal Reserve Chairman Alan Greenspan.

> to the others. They often learn each other's languages and about each other's special habits, and up to a point accept and respect each other's cultural identities.[40]

Homilists do this to signal that they accept and respect the generational identities of those present in the Sunday assembly.

While not commonly applied, the intentional effort to understand and connect with the everyday language and culture of those in the congregation is not an historically new intuition. Gleaning the rich history of Christian preachers, we find Martin Luther adapting the Scriptures into the German vernacular; his church following suit with turning contemporary drinking songs into popular religious hymns. Methodists John and Charles Wesley agreed "to become more vile" by preaching in the fields and town plazas in order to meet the common folk in their milieu. Salvation Army General William Booth infamously asked: "Why should the Devil have all the good tunes?"[41] More recent times have offered the media-savvy preacher Catholic Bishop Fulton Sheen successfully reaching out to both white and blue-collar intergenerational audiences through radio and television.

When preachers effectively pass between generational speech communities, they demonstrate what is known as *communicative competence*.[42] Paraphrasing Johnson, I would define this concept as: a *preacher's* sensitivity to the people, places and activities of *a particular generation*. Far from a laundry list of semantic "do's and don'ts," communicative competence suggests the ability to judge accurately the appropriate and relevant uses of language in a given cultural situation. Preachers need to appreciate and develop such competence within the culture of generation if they hope to preach effectively, collectively and simultaneously to the varied generations represented in their Sunday assembly. In effect, then, the culture of generation influences direct communication by explicitly impacting the shape, sound and substance of the homilist's message.

[40] Teun A. Van Dijk, "Discourse as Interaction in Society," in *Discourse as Social Interaction,* 2, Teun A. Van Dijk, ed. (London: Sage Publications, 1997) 34.

[41] Charles Trueheart, "Welcome to the Next Church," *The Atlantic Monthly* (August 1996) 44.

[42] Johnson, 41. Johnson explains: "To use a language and to interact with others through a coherent discourse require the acquisition, development, and application of what has been termed *communicative competence,* which is the knowledge system underlying the appropriate use of language in context."

Speaking to different generations in one seating challenges preachers to continually examine what communicative competence in the pulpit truly means. Communication scholar Brian Spitzberg defines competent communication as "interaction that is perceived as effective in fulfilling certain rewarding objectives in a way that is also appropriate to the context in which the interaction occurs."[43] Those contexts, according to Teun Van Dijk, are socially based mental constructs, or models in memory:

> Since meaning and other discourse properties are also mentally managed, this also explains the vital link between discourse and context: as subjective representations, mental models of contexts may thus directly monitor the production and comprehension of talk and text. Indeed, without such subjectivity of language users and their minds, the "same" social contexts would have the same effect on all language users in the same situation, which they obviously have not.[44]

Yet we preachers can so often preach in a way that presumes one standard approach in the minds and hearts of the "language users" that sit in our pews. This conscious or unconscious assumption renders our message ineffective and us less than credible. Why? The preaching doesn't fully appreciate the many symbolic and linguistic differences inherent among the generations.

Van Dijk takes us to the heart of the matter: *When one preaches, what does the congregation hear?* More pointedly, what do the arguably five to six different generations each hear? Certainly, they do not hear the same thing or in the same way. Preachers have historically proceeded as though the very opposite were true. They have tended to either offer a one-size-fits-all approach that is oblivious or dismissive of the distinctive models of memory held by each generation or have sought the half-measure remedy of separating younger generations of worshipers during the proclamation and preaching of the Word. In a liturgical moment that is ultimately about unifying the faithful, worshipers are divided. This is not communicative competence that connects and unifies but homiletic incompetence that divides and stratifies!

[43] Brian H. Spitzberg, "Communication Competence: Measures of Perceived Effectiveness" in *A Handbook for the Study of Human Communication,* Charles H. Tardy, ed. (Norwood, N.J.: Ablex).

[44] Van Dijk, 16.

What I coin *intergenerational communicative competence* requires an intentional incorporation of aspects of different generations' models of memory in weekly Sunday preaching. Unfortunately, too little attention has been paid to this topic in Catholic circles, much less the urgent, fundamental need to effectively preach to the growing multi-generational nature of our Sunday gatherings.[45]

Communication scholars suggest that communication competence can be further expanded to encompass the concept of culture: "Cultural competence is conduct which is appropriate and effective for the particular identity being adopted at the time in the particular situation."[46] Culture, according to Saint Louis University Professor Karla Scott, "provides individuals with a blueprint for living and interpreting their environment."[47] Might we not then be able to assume that a generation's self-understanding is one of the major influences on how that blueprint evolves? If this assumption is correct, then enhancing the effectiveness of preaching in a multi-generational gathering requires the preacher to interweave qualities descriptive of each generation's worldview at strategic points throughout the homily.[48]

These generational motifs, skillfully and strategically placed, draw the varied generations in as they hear that the preacher knows who they are culturally amid the obvious age diversity. Multi-generational preachers then achieve "communicative competence in choosing what to say, as well as how and when to say it."[49] The motive behind their choice is the desire to speak individually and effectively to each generation while preaching collectively to all. The aim of intergenerational communicative competence is accomplished when the preacher is sensitive and respectful of generational diversity as a legitimate cultural dynamic.

[45] This concept will be explored later.

[46] Mary Jane Collier, "Cultural and Intercultural Communication Competence: Current Approaches and Directions for Future Research" in *International Journal of Intercultural Relations,* no. 13 (1989) 296.

[47] Karla Scott, "Strategies of Cultural Competence: Language Use in HIV Prevention Programs for African American Communities" in paper presented at the 127th Annual Meeting of the National Communication Association, Seattle, November 11, 2000.

[48] These worldviews are shaped by their subculture's particular norms, values, habits and special language variations /vocabulary.

[49] Romaine, "Language in Society/Society in Language," 31.

The growing phenomenon of the popularly labeled "mega-churches" movement offers creative and valuable insight on this latter point. Movement leaders such as Pastors Leith Anderson and George Hunter, respectively, emphasize "reading . . . [and] translating the culture," and that "it is necessary for a church to become culturally indigenousness to its 'mission field.'"[50] When intergenerational preaching is taken to its logical conclusion, does it not call for a seriously adherent preacher to become culturally or *generationally indigenous*? Is not that the heart of the challenge?

Communicative competence as well as homiletic integrity would seem to demand it. As Hunter reasons: "When the church's communication forms are alien to the host population, they may never perceive that Christianity's God is for people like them."[51] If preachers don't know how to speak with the varied generations they view from the pulpit each Sunday, if their homiletic preparation does not include an exegesis of those assembled, then competence, let alone the transformative communication for which preaching strives, is not even in the ballpark!

What can we now say of homiletics as it relates to language and culture, specifically, the subculture of generation? Preaching is a persuasive form of discourse that ought to be structured and oriented to the preferences of each generation's symbols and language. It is a *rhetorical system*[52] through which the preacher persuades, influences and appeals to another. One of the best examples of this is the *call-response* sermon, a rhetorical style unique to African-American discourse. In call-response, the congregation verbally responds during the sermon encouraging or discouraging the direction of the preacher's message. These responses are not necessarily restricted to the preacher but can occur between the members of the congregation as well.[53] Thus, any form of discourse is action. "People say or write in order to accomplish social, political or cultural acts in various local contexts as well as within the broader frameworks of societal structure and culture."[54] One of those broader cultural and structural frameworks is

[50] Trueheart, 43.

[51] Ibid., 43.

[52] Johnson, 37. Rhetorical systems are those vehicles through which "individuals appeal to one another and seek to persuade or influence." Examples are religious or political speeches, marketing slogans, or even social justice mantras.

[53] Ibid., 150.

[54] Van Dijk, 34.

generation. Therefore, preaching is a speech act because it both *says* and *does*.[55]

Multi-generational preaching is a specific genre or form of social action that engages both text and talk.[56] This engagement is an organized and structured effort in order to influence generations through the subculture of age. By text and talk we mean not only *what* is said but also *how* it is said. We also mean that which is mentally and thoughtfully conveyed through the spoken word. Marshall McLuhan's famous dictum seems very appropriate: "The medium is the message."[57] While his context was the television industry, the application is nonetheless genuine because McLuhan, like Van Dijk, wants us "to think about the nature of the spoken word versus the nature of the written text."[58]

Intergenerational preaching is, therefore, an argument for the meeting of *cognition* and *context*.[59] The concept of cognition refers to the subjectivity language users bring to an interaction because of their age. The language that preachers must present is simultaneously the language of the speech communities from five or six different generations. The diverse and collective nature of the intergenerational gathering is also a significant and influential element of the context. Van Dijk emphasizes that "discourses are a structural part of their contexts and their respective structures mutually and continually influence each other."[60] For the intergenerational homilist, these mutually influencing structures are the various assembled generations. As such, they reflect novel opportunities and implications when preaching to varied age groupings in one setting. If preachers acknowledge the multiple generations that exist in the societal microcosm of the Sunday assembly and also appreciably consider the linguistic and symbolic differences that characterize the assembly, they

> can . . . express the gospel so that each generation can hear the promise and demand of the gospel in their own language, and so that a generation's consciousness can be shaped by the gospel.[61]

[55] Ibid., 42.
[56] Ibid., 164.
[57] Jay Rosen, "Playing the Primary Chords," *Harper's Magazine* (March 1992) 22.
[58] Ibid., 22.
[59] Van Dijk, 16.
[60] Ibid., 15.
[61] Allen, 399.

C. The Dance of Meaning

A number of questions remain. What shapes consciousness? What is the relationship between meaning and language? How accurate is the common assumption that the latter transmits and communicates the former? It has been a popular phrase within human potential workshops to speak of human beings as "meaning-making machines." If that is true, how does the human person "make meaning"? What is the role of language and symbol? Finally, what is the influence of *generational identity* that forms the construction of that meaning?

Gee offers extensive reflection in relation to these questions. He disabuses us of the readily accepted notion that language is first and foremost about communicating meaning. "Learning to mean and learning to language"[62] while related, are separate undertakings. Language is not a series of meanings but a fluid grammatical form or pattern learned from childhood, one that is perennially at the mercy of the ebb and flow of social culture and personal history.

Languages are "*social possessions,*" the function of which is not just to provide information but also to act as "a device to think and feel with . . . a device with which to signal and negotiate social identity."[63]

I spoke earlier of the preacher's challenge of negotiating social boundaries that are also generational in nature, especially in light of differing generational dialects. That negotiation is taken up in the assumed, but not always happy or solid, marriage between language and meaning, the two linguistic gladiators at the heart of social *and generational* identity. Political consultant and ad man Tony Schwartz corroborates Gee's assertion of the surreptitious match between meaning and language in his *The Responsive Chord:*

> A listener or viewer brings far more information to the communication event than a communicator can put into his [her] . . . message. The communicator's problem, then, is not to get stimuli across, or even to package his [her] stimuli so they can be understood and absorbed. Rather, he [the communicator] must deeply understand the kinds of information and experiences stored in his [her] audience, the patterning of this information, and the interactive resonance process whereby stimuli evoke stored information.[64]

[62] Gee, 71.
[63] Ibid., 76.
[64] Tony Schwartz quoted in Rosen, 22–23.

Both Schwartz and Gee reject the common notion that the purpose of communication is to provide information/meaning from point A to point B along some imaginary highway. Some have referred to this idea as the "transportation"[65] metaphor.[66] It would seem that Gee's conclusion of how "meaning is made" would resonate with Schwartz's own thinking above. Gee defines the production of meaning (what speakers and writers do)

> as choices about exclusions (and inclusions) and assumptions about contexts made on a certain basis, and the comprehension of meaning (what hearers and readers do) as guesses about these choices and assumptions.[67]

Gee encapsulates in this definition the other two principles he proposes as central to the production of meaning: the *guessing principle* and the *context principle*.[68] These two principles are distinct but related. The former asserts that people can only guess at what they and others mean by the words chosen in a given interaction, while the latter maintains that those guesses are directed and influenced by the context in which they are made. Isn't this also Van Dijk's point when he suggests that mental models of context play a role in monitoring the production of text and talk? This only reinforces the notion that discourse can never be separated from context anymore then "meaning-making" can be separated from language choices in a given interaction.

Schwartz's *responsive chord* theory harkens back to Johnson's point regarding credible code-switching. This technique requires explicit knowledge of the cultures from which one is shifting back and forth. Like Johnson, Schwartz too would seem to want to encourage "the communicator" in his scenario to consider the *social semiotics* at play. In other words, what patterns of systematic social meaning *already below the surface* inform the audience's perceptions, preferences and prejudices? Schwartz's thinking also appears to argue for a level of communicative competence on the part of the speaker. If "the communicator" were to *hit* the responsive chord already "out there" in the audience's experience, "the communicator" would certainly seem to

[65] Ibid., 22.

[66] Gee, 78. Instead of this "transportation" metaphor, Gee coins these: the *container/conveyor metaphor.*

[67] Ibid., 82.

[68] Ibid., 82.

need to understand and draw upon the underlying knowledge system of appropriate, contextual language usage.

The contributions of those cited above resonate with authorities from other academic and cross-disciplinary fields. The means of communication have dramatically and definitively changed. If preachers hope to speak to future generations, they must acknowledge that reality up-front and without ambiguity. Author Robert Weber captures the tone of that expansion of communication:

> The new revolutions in science, philosophy and communications —in all areas of life—are shifting us toward the affirmation of new values. We live, science says, in an expanding universe; we are, philosophy states, in an interrelationship with all things; and we increasingly communicate through visual and symbolic means.[69]

D. Conclusion

I said earlier that intergenerational preaching is a form of discourse and more precisely, a speech act. Gee recommends questions when one is deciding "the form in which to enact a speech act."[70] These questions are applicable to the discernment needed by a homilist preparing to preach to a multi-generational assembly:

- How socially close or distant am I and the [particular generation]?
- How much or little power does the [particular generation] have over me?
- How significant (to me, to the [generation]) is the act I want to engage in?
- How much emphasis do you and I (and our [generations]) place on positive face needs as against negative face needs in circumstances like this one?
- How does the context *I am* [as a particular generation] affect the answers to the above questions?

[69] Robert Weber quoted in Roberto, 1.
[70] Gee, 98.

- Has the [particular generation] or would the [particular generation] compute the answers to the above questions the same as I in a circumstance like the one we are in?[71]

Wrestling with these questions is an inherent part of the intergenerational preacher's preparation. It is important for homilists to know how socially and culturally close they are to a particular age group in order to compensate appropriately and effectively. The homiletic challenge is not only discerning *what* generation to reach, but also *how* to reach them.

Another concern is the way that preachers understand their place of moral authority among the varying generations. That authority affects how boldly or diminutively the exegetical and pastoral approach will be. The degree of importance homilists attach to connecting with several or all of the age groupings present in the congregation impacts how they engage in the speech act of preaching. The self-awareness of the preachers regarding the effect their perceived presence as the vestured, officially sanctioned, proclaimer and preacher of the Word has on the congregation's diverse ages is also crucial and relevant.

In their document *Fulfilled in Your Hearing*, the U.S. Catholic Bishops speak of the power of language in a way that resonates with the points summarized above. One of the most important, and specifically human, ways in which faith is communicated to individuals and communities is through language. The way we speak about our world expresses the way we think about it and interpret it. One of the reasons we speak about our world at all is to share our vision of the world with others. "The preacher is a Christian especially charged with sharing the Christian vision of the world as the creation of a loving God. . . . If the words of Scripture are divinely inspired, as we believe them to be, then divine inspiration must be at work when those words are made alive and contemporary to the believing community in and through our ministry."[72]

Understanding the *social possessions* of each age group to whom the homilist will preach is critical in navigating the unpredictable waters of generational mindsets. Yet, the generations need not remain unchartered waters for the preacher determined to set sail among them

[71] Ibid., 98. The original questions used "hearers" in place of "particular generations." The italics in the fifth bullet are mine.

[72] *Fulfilled in Your Hearing,* 18, 11.

in the seaworthy ship of God's universal Word. Before setting out on those unpredictable waves, what can preachers learn from those who negotiate their height, depth, length and breath as the part of their everyday livelihood? We now turn to marketers, who can teach something to preachers about sailing successfully among the generations through a homiletic application of modern market segmentation.

What the Preacher Can Learn from the Marketer

4

Some would think it strange to compare the two seemingly diverse fields of religion and economics. There is, however, a long and traditional connection between them. Friedrich Hayek's *The Fatal Conceit* and Max Weber's *The Protestant Ethic and the Spirit of Capitalism* are both respective examples of current and former debate on the relationship between economics and religion.[1] Thinkers like Edmund Bruke and Francis Fukuyama have "reflected not only on the morality of the marketplace . . . but on the wider question of the kind of society that gives rise to and is able to sustain a market economy."[2] Weber, as well as Catholic scholar Michael Novak, have impressed upon the minds of their audiences the notion that religion was a force that shaped our modern economy. It appears now that the marketplace with its attendant strategies could contribute to the *churchyard* wherein the homilist toils with strategies to reach an increasingly intergenerational assembly. Indeed, as opposed as marketing theory and homiletics may seem at first glance, preaching can learn from a qualified market segmentation theory. A brief discussion of the approach of market segmentation and its proponents will help clarify this learning.

Wendell Smith, in his groundbreaking article of the mid-1950s, established himself, bar none, as the "Father of Market Segmentation." Smith introduces the terms and ideas foundational to his approach in the following:

[1] Sacks, 23–24. The morality of the marketplace is "what we nowadays call 'businesses ethics.'"

[2] Ibid., 23.

> Segmentation . . . is based upon developments on the demand side of the market and represents a rational and more precise adjustment of product and marketing effort to consumer or user requirements. In the language of the economist, segmentation is *disaggregative* in its effects and tends to bring about recognition of several demand schedules where only one was recognized before.[3]

The essence of market segmentation is the recognition of smaller markets within the virtual labyrinth of the mass market. By *disaggregative* Smith is referring to the variables inherent in demand schedules (consumers grouped according to higher or lower demands for a particular product). In today's marketing practice, these variables have been broadened to include any combination of what are known as the Four Ps: *product, price, placement* and *promotion,* which comprise what is known as the *marketing mix.*[4] Developing an effective marketing mix is an exercise in creative manipulation of the Four Ps to meet the taste and needs of the consumer as precisely as possible.

Frederick Winter, while affirming the continuing validity of Smith's definition, suggests a more comprehensive understanding that expands to include the concept of *cost-benefit segmentation*:

> Market segmentation is the recognition that groups and subsegments differ with respect to properties that suggest that different marketing mixes might be used to appeal to different groups. These subsegments may then be aggregated if the reduction in cost exceeds the reduction in benefits (revenues). This aggregation is based on the fact that both subsegments respond most to the same marketing mix.[5]

Market segmentation attempts to strategically target and divide broad select markets into smaller, more manageable subgroups through applying the most cost-effective and appealing marketing mix to a particular segment of the population. It is the shaping and refining of communication to best meet the needs and interest of the specific

[3] Wendell R. Smith, "Product Differentiation and Market Segmentation as Alternative Marketing Strategies," *Journal of Marketing* 20 (July 1956) 5.

[4] Wilkie, 88.

[5] Frederick Winter, "Marketing Segmentation: A Tactical Approach," in *Marketing Manager: A Comprehensive Reader,* Jadish N. Sheth and Dennis E. Garret, eds. (Cincinnati: South-Western Publishing Co., 1986) 429–30.

subgroup. How effectively this is achieved determines the competitive advantage of one marketer and brand product over another. There are three key steps in the process:

- Identifying segments
- Selecting particular segments to target
- Creating marketing mixes aimed at target segments[6]

In the first step, specific groups of consumers are identified as solid potential for a particular marketing initiative. Determining what particular segment to target in consideration of the company business interests and goals is the second step. The third step involves decisions on how best to coordinate the *product, price, placement* and *promotion* for those targeted segments to ensure an effective marketing mix precisely adapted to the group of consumers it is designed to reach. The corollary to these steps is a set of three basic criteria that ensure a genuine market segment. The search is for a customer grouping that

- Can be identified
- Will behave differently from other groups
- Will be responsive to an efficient marketing mix[7]

The most important aspect of the first requirement, identifying the customer grouping, is to ask the questions: What are consumers' personal characteristics? How do they behave routinely? What benefits do they seek consistently?[8] Segmenting by personal characteristics allows marketers to establish and distinguish customer groupings according to targeted divisions. While there are many types of segmentation,[9] I will concern myself in this book with only one: *demographic*. Here, demographic profiles of consumers are developed according to gender, age, ethnicity, occupation, and income or education.[10]

[6] Wilkie, 88.

[7] Ibid., 88–89.

[8] Ibid., 91.

[9] Examples of basic segmentation approaches most utilized today include: demographic, media exposure, life-style/psychographic, geographic.

[10] Wilkie, 92.

Once individual segments are identified, they are defined further by the benefits they seek and evaluated according to both behavioral and personality differences. This behavioral data provides a further classification by which segments can be understood and for which marketing mixes can be designed.

Smith's concluding comment at the beginning of this section that "only one was recognized before" is a reference to the perceived monopoly of the idea of the mass market: the emphasis on broad circulation to undifferentiated audiences. I say, "perceived," because, in truth, segmentation has been around as long as the competition for goods and services. Drawing upon social historian Susan Strasser, Joseph Turow says: "The seeds of 'market segmentation and targeted promotion' were sown in the first quarter of the twentieth-century as advertisers and their agencies looked for ways to expand their product's reach."[11] The only thing that is new is a more sophisticated analysis of the ever-developing theories around consumer behavior. As one author has put it, from its so-called "introduction" in the 1950s to now, "market segmentation could be judged to have shifted in status from an art to a science."[12]

That shift came about in the late 1970s. The novelty at that time was not the specialized appeal to targeted audiences but "the emergence of target marketing as a hot, hip, even central strategy after decades of being considered a relatively marginal part of the national ad industry's thinking."[13]

Thanks to technology, segmentation is the most popular tool of all marketing ideology and practice because it allows for alternative perspectives on the market through moving away from grouping all consumers together as though they were equal in their tastes and preferences. It further allows for separating consumers as distinctive, smaller entities with different likes and dislikes who should be approached in different ways. From its perch, both the marketer and the consumer can be studied and understood. The degree to which marketers increase their knowledge of consumers defines the extent of a business' competitive advantage in the marketplace.

[11] Joseph Turow, *Breaking Up America* (Chicago: The University of Chicago Press, 1997) 28.

[12] Peter R. Dickson and James L. Ginter, "Market Segmentation, Product Differentiation, and Marketing Strategy" in *Journal of Marketing* 51, no. 2 (April 1987) 1.

[13] Turow, 19.

The Nielsen Company, famous for its television ratings system, is a good example of working for this advantage.[14] Not long after the inception of television, the company began to use its ratings system to collect information on the American families whose habits it had been monitoring. Through the families studied, "advertisers could obtain ratings of programs according to categories such as gender, age, educational stature, urban or rural location, and other factors [which meet] human wants more accurately than the competition."[15] This is a corollary strategy, espoused by Smith, that is known as *product differentiation*:

> the bending of demand to the will of supply . . . [which] results from the desire to establish a kind of equilibrium in the market by bringing about adjustment of market demand to supply conditions favorable to the seller.[16]

In other words, the idea is to continually manipulate the entire marketing mix[17] in a more precise manner than the competition to draw more accurately upon the preference of the consumer. No business wants to lower the quality of the product, so it must focus upon and accentuate clearly the differences between its own company and competitors. Lines do vary, however, according to price, features, and quality.

A. How Market Segmentation Can Help the Preacher

How is market segmentation theory adaptable for preaching, specifically in addressing the problems mentioned earlier in chapter 1? In the language of the intergenerational preacher, segmentation is the methodology by which preachers exegete their congregation. Through this exegesis, they analyze the congregation and develop a homiletic strategy that recognizes the existence of several different generational viewpoints where before only one was assumed and addressed. The precise adjustment that occurs within the exegetical process, both biblical and congregational, is what *develops* the product

[14] Ibid., 25.
[15] Ibid., 25.
[16] Smith, 5.
[17] The Four Ps: *product, price, placement,* and *promotion*.

[Word of God] with a deliberate marketing effort [selected style of delivery: choice of words, images, and examples] that *communicates* the product in order to meet consumer or user requirements [the multi-generational assembly's self-understanding of its own needs and desired benefits].

Earlier I stated that the Church already attempts a generational segmentation by separating children from adults during the Scripture readings or through specialized young adult celebrations of the Eucharist. While these segmentation efforts suggest a growing inter-generational awareness from the pulpit, they attempt to solve one problem by creating another. Separation of the varied generations for more effective worship is antithetical to the unity worship ultimately intends.

Interestingly enough, the Church has struggled with this issue before. There is a biblical and historical basis for the heart of my proposal: a homiletic approach that embraces a qualified segmentation based on the subculture of generation. It is an approach that simultaneously recognizes and speaks to distinctive cultures while preaching to the whole. It thereby recognizes and endorses a coexistence of these cultures made possible by the universal truth of the message preached. No less than early Christianity's greatest preacher wrestled with this very dilemma. St. Paul was consumed with his mission to bring the Gentiles into the Church, even calling himself "The Apostle to the Gentiles." How could they be recognized as legitimate coheirs of the Kingdom of God along with the Jews?

In his insightful work *Paul Among Jews and Gentiles,* Krister Stendahl sheds new light on the implications of God's revelation that the Jews are not the sole heirs to the Kingdom. "As a Jew, [Paul] had grown accustomed to dividing humankind into two parts."[18] Stendahl challenges the long held interpretation that Paul's Epistle to the Romans is primarily about the doctrine of justification by faith. The latter was but a secondary theme to serve Paul's true theme, the relationship between the Jews and Gentiles. Yet, the Church, according to Stendahl, *marketed* the wrong interpretation. Paul was trying to speak to two audiences at the same time. The doctrine of justification by faith was only a side comment on why he was even bothering to make this effort. Paul's overriding purpose in his epistle was to preach in a way

[18] Krister Stendahl, *Paul Among Jews and Gentiles* (Philadelphia: Fortress Press, 1976) 1.

that would unite two very distinctive cultures in the one universal truth of Jesus Christ. To achieve this delicate task, Paul emphasized a different focus of the Good News for each particular community while consistently preaching the same truth: God's unconditional love and constant fidelity. For example:

- For Israel in conflict, the good news is the announcement that God caused the enemy to flee.
- For Israel in exile, the good news is that God is beginning the homecoming.
- For a world choking in the grip of Satan, the good news is that Jesus is the stronger one.
- For a world alienated from the gods, the good news is that reconciliation with God has been revealed in Jesus Christ.[19]

Another example is the dispute over baptism that Paul addresses in Galatians 3:26-29. His concern is to help the Jews and Greeks see that they are one in Christ (Col 3:10-11) through baptism (Rom 6:3-11), and thus, it follows logically, heirs of Abraham.[20] This is just one of any number of famous "stumbling blocks" (Rom 14:13) that threatens Paul's exhausting effort to keep the growing, but divisive, early Church from erupting.

The fragmented church at Corinth offers additional examples beyond baptism. From the eating of idol meats, to women's roles in the liturgy, to appropriate dress, Paul is besieged (1 Cor 10:1-17). Yet, his message in the midst of these divisions is consistent: unity in the truth of Jesus Christ.

The tightrope Paul continually straddled is reflected in his writings as well as in his preaching. His correspondence was not casual chitchat but most often tough and penetrating. Theologian Marion Soards claims Paul's letters were a calculated, strategic part of his whole missionary approach; indeed, "for Paul the letter was an instrument of his apostleship."[21] He wielded that instrument mightily,

[19] Ronald J. Allen, *Preaching for Growth* (St. Louis: CBP Press, 1988) 11.

[20] Galatians 3:26-29: An appeal to baptismal equality, in footnote in *The New Oxford Annotated Bible,* NRSA (New York: Oxford University Press, 1991) 267.

[21] Marion L. Soards, *The Apostle Paul: An Introduction to His Writings and Teaching* (New York: Paulist Press, 1987) 32.

addressing specific issues in specific churches that he had founded. Paul's struggle of separateness and who is right and wrong unfortunately continues today.

The growing success of the contemporary mega-church movement, which some interpret as an indictment against mainline denominations, chronicles a similar challenge. Episcopalian writer Charles Trueheart explores this phenomenon in his article, "Welcome to the Next Church." First, he makes the general observation that

> Social institutions that once held civic life together—schools, families, governments, companies, neighborhoods, and even old-style churches—are not what they used to be. The new congregations are reorganizing religious life to fill the void. The Next Church in its fully realized state can be the clearest approximation of community, and perhaps the most important civic structure, that a whole generation is likely to have known or likely to find anywhere in an impersonal, transient nation.[22]

Second, he states familiar statistics that make a shocking and effective case that mainline denominational churches are hemorrhaging if not on life-support systems.[23] While thousands upon thousands of believing Americans still flock to church each Sunday, they are most likely not attending the church of their parents or grandparents but "The Next Church." This church is not tied down to the ritual, doctrinal or architectural trappings of the traditional Church. Rather, these churches are freed to pursue innovative worship and community building. Trueheart notes that moving beyond these historically formalistic and ritually set boundaries suggests not just a redefinition of sacred space and communal worship for the traditional Sunday gathering but of secular communities as well.

Trueheart touches upon themes of strong civic structures that the French scholar Alexis de Tocqueville lauded two centuries ago as the very strength of America. At the same time, authors such as Harvard Professor Robert Putnam lament that these structures are in serious

[22] Trueheart, 38.

[23] Ibid., 38. "Half of all American Protestant churches have fewer then seventy-five congregants." That makes sense when one considers only 12 percent of all church-going Americans (about half) regularly attend our country's 400,000 churches. Inner cities churches are closing their doors at the rate of fifty a week.

decline. In Putnam's popular *Bowling Alone*[24] he suggests that the decline in league bowling is an apt metaphor for the direction of American communal participation.

The particularly poignant American tension between individualism and civic involvement and the weakened sense of communal responsibility and commitment were also central themes of the 1980s bestseller *Habits of the Heart* (the title was coined by Tocqueville).[25] The Next Church is clearly and strategically committed to filling this void by offering a significant response to this decline. Its organizational structure makes it well poised to do so!

Known as mega-churches precisely because their congregations can number up to ten thousand,[26] this movement seeks to build institutional commitment through a *product* that not only offers contemporary worship freed of the "old ways" but a "Monday through Sunday service center." An official statement of purpose by the Fellowship of Las Clinas, in Irving, Texas, is telling:

> We exist to reach up—which is worship (expressing love to God); to reach out—which is evangelism (or sharing Christ with others); and to reach in—which is discipleship (becoming fully devoted members of Christ).[27]

"Reaching up, reaching out and reaching in" is a full-time, seven-day-a-week affair. Beyond Sunday worship, these churches offer opportunities to live one's faith by getting involved in evangelism and volunteer efforts during the week. Those opportunities are laid out each Sunday not only in practical applications made by the preacher in the sermon but also in hallways lined with booths offering everything. Typical examples are an AA group or a prayer group for those who clean the church each week. Others include volunteer pools for evangelization purposes to pools who offer auto-mechanic support for members. These and other programs and services are tailored

[24] "The Price of Democracy," editorial in *Saint Louis Post Dispatch* (December 3, 2000).

[25] Robert N. Bellah, Richard Madsen, William M. Sullivan, Ann Swidler, and Steven M. Tipton, *Habits of the Heart* (New York: Harper & Row, 1985) 37. Tocqueville's "habits of the heart" refer to basic democratic mores and principles upon which "the American experiment" was founded and maintained.

[26] Trueheart, 38.

[27] Ibid., 46.

for all generations. This is not only the principle of segmentation at its most creative but its most cost-effective. As Trueheart observes:

> Big congregations endow a church with critical mass, which makes possible . . . formidable volunteer pools, and thus the capacity to *diversify* almost infinitely in order to develop new "product lines" that meet the congregation's needs and involve members in unpaid service.[28]

At first blush this may seem a bit much, "an unseemly market-driven approach to building the kingdom of God."[29] Yet, these churches have identified and selected unsatisfied or unchurched segments of the population[30] and given them a place for meaningful religious commitment. They have created marketing mixes that cater to their *customer's* personal growth issues and communal need to belong. They offer a product that is malleable to their *consumer,* a price that is considered reasonable in terms of cost and benefits, a placement that respects varying generational needs and issues, and a part in promotion through the church emphasis on evangelization (expanding membership).

While valid questions can be and are being raised about the theological limits of an ecclesial approach that focuses on identifying and giving people what they want in terms of religious experience, the mega-churches movement should not be quickly dismissed. The fact is that too many of those who sit in the mainline denominational pews each Sunday are feeling spiritually disenfranchised or even spiritually dead. The Next Church is a clarion call to mainline churches to wake up and recognize the sobering reality that people are not being fed and are going to places where they will be fed.

The message seems clear. Protestant theologian Marva Dawn's comment at an annual Academy of Homiletics meeting captures it: "Generation X is looking for a Christ who breaks down barriers."[31] The age diversity of those drawn to the mega-churches suggests that Gen-X is not alone in that desire nor in the determination to vote that feeling with their feet!

[28] Ibid., 38.

[29] Ibid., 38.

[30] Many are nominal or renounced Catholics.

[31] Marva Dawn, Academy of Homiletics Annual Meeting, Dallas, Texas, December 2, 2000.

B. Contributions and Limitations of Market Segmentation

Now that we have explored market segmentation's potential adaptation to homiletics, it is important to delineate the former's strengths and weaknesses.

1. *Contributions*

The marketer searches for a market. The preacher has one: the congregation. The marketer attempts to produce depth in his/her market position by effectively defining and penetrating new and diverse segments. Homilists, if they wish to pursue the opportunity, may be readily credible with *varied segments* as well because they are already consistently present and identified with a particular parish. Pastors must develop strategies to increase the depth of commitment in various segments of the congregation.

Similarly, as preachers they must adjust communication styles to achieve this depth in the assembly. This is akin to finding the right *marketing mix*: an exercise in the creative manipulation of the Four Ps mentioned earlier. For the strategic goals of the preacher, *Price* is concerned with not only communicating the cost of the gospel message but the cost of not having a life rooted in the Gospel.[32] *Place* refers to the context in which the message is communicated. How is the message situated; where is a particular point "placed" in the scope of the homily? Where and when is the homily delivered? *Promotion* suggests the issue of effective communication of the message: What is the best delivery vehicle? What approach can most effectively be used? The *Product* was described earlier. It is then incumbent upon the preacher to skillfully and subtly interweave these individual marketing mixes together to create an intergenerational homily that speaks to the identified generations in a collective context.

Parishes, like markets, do not consist of people with homogeneous needs. Drawing from the work of cultural anthropologists, Tisdale explains that people can be viewed from three valid perspectives:

- Like all others (sharing certain universals with the whole human race)

[32] Here, of course, the price is expected to be high if the product is valuable. We are not, after all, talking "bargain shopping."

- Like no others (having distinctive traits that mark them as individuals), and
- Like some others (sharing cultural traits with a particular group of people)

Each of these realities has significant implications for the preaching event.[33] Preachers need to know to whom they are speaking. Marketers identify and define particular segments by product use: Classic Coke users, Diet Coke or Caffeine-free Coke users. Analogously, preachers can categorize the different age groups represented in their pews according to generational segments described in the earlier table. This division of generational groupings is a form of demographic segmentation. The objective of segmentation for the preacher and the marketer is the same: to adapt a specific marketing mix to the requirement of a particular market. Thus, segmentation becomes a new aspect of congregational analysis.

Let us consider an analysis of these generations in relation to Table 1. When preparing homilies, preachers should keep the following generational segmentation in mind as it will make a significant difference in the style and substance of their preaching. In terms of substance, it could easily provide the missing connection we spoke of earlier in Chapter 1. As for style, strategic utilization of the following generational profiles allows for flexibility and originality in attempting to reach each generation:

- ***Builders:*** The preacher can draw them in through emphasizing that the gospel message creates internal security and an external secure world. The preacher's challenge to the Builders' personal growth is that security is rooted in God, not in preserving the status quo. Sometimes, for God's purposes, "the apple cart" has to be disturbed. Builders have a "can-do" attitude and respond well to calls to repentance. Linear by nature, they like clear, point-by-point homilies.
- ***Silent:*** This generation is known as "silent" because "much of their energy is spent in responding to the Builders ahead of them and the Boomers behind them."[34] From the sidelines and away from the spotlight other generations have shared, the

[33] Tisdale, 11.
[34] Allen, "Preaching to Different Generations," 377.

Silent Generation exhibits a genuine moral and social conscience. Their natural impulse resonates with a preacher's call to demonstrate faith through action. A homilist who isn't afraid to assert that such faith costs something challenges this generation. This generation believes that cost is worth it if their efforts serve as a reconciling bridge for others to cross. They like a conversational style from the pulpit.

- ***Baby Boomers:*** The preacher attracts this group of "personal meaning seekers" through references to and programs for their children. Boomers are very family-oriented and idealistic. They want to make the world a better, more just place for themselves, their children, and society's most vulnerable. Boomers are driven to excel and look for the same from their preacher. They don't mind being challenged to a distinctive vision and standard but do not respond to autocratic or authoritarian styles. They most appreciate a homilist who is warm and communicative.
- ***Generation X:*** By temperament more suspicious, Xers are not as moved to act on their deep convictions as the Silent and Boomer generations. They are spiritual but more relaxed about religion than preceding generations, not wanting to commit to any one viewpoint. As a postmodern generation, they don't automatically grant the homilist authority because he/she steps into the pulpit. Whereas earlier generations want to know how to live their beliefs, Xers want to know why they should believe the claims of this faith over another. Having grown up in an electronic age, they respond to images and storytelling in a homily. A preacher can also capture their attention through relationship metaphors. The best preacher to them is not an intellectual apologist, but an honest and authentic human being willing to share his/her own struggles about Gospel living.[35]
- ***Millennial:*** Like the preceding generation, the Millennial Generation seeks a relevant message from the Good News that addresses real, everyday life. Also nonlinear and interactive like Generation X, they best receive the preacher's message through their use of practical images and visuals. They differ in their intellectual and emotional openness. Preachers have their confidence, not through the authority of title but through a general

[35] Ibid., 376–400.

> openness to their contribution. The homilist who communicates in a way that helps them explore and discover new connections between the Gospel and their lives will receive a warm hearing.[36]

The above represents a broad brushstroke. As Allen reminds us: "A cohort is not a monolith . . . some persons, in fact, are transgenerational."[37] This calls upon the preacher to stay abreast not only of the evolving nature of the generations present in the assembly, but aware of the complex individuals who comprise them.[38]

2. *Limitations*

Here the marketer and the homilist part ways. The truth of the Gospel as the product of the preacher can never be adjusted in itself, but its "packaging" can be customized so as to be more favorable to the interests of the hearer and/or the preacher. The truth of Scripture is not a variable in this equation and must be preached in its full veracity in season and out of season. It is true, however, that the preacher is able to adjust the communication methods, style of delivery, linguistic choices, and anecdotal selections in order to optimize interest[39] of those hearing the Word. Unlike the marketer, however, preachers seek to identify various segments of the congregation out of concern for the Christian truth of the Gospel.

The final goals of marketing and homiletic strategies are ultimately different. On the one hand, the marketer attempts to reach a particular, unique and optimal aggregate of consumers so that their advertisers can make money in the most efficient, low-cost and high-benefits way possible. The more "targeted audiences" shrink, the more valuable they become.[40] In fact, the market's breastplate could easily read: "Divide and conquer." In the mid-1990s, MTV deliberately cast the cable series *Beavis and Butt-head* as a signature show that would

[36] Roberto, 14–15.

[37] Allen, "Preaching to Different Generations," 370.

[38] A cautionary note needs to be sounded at this point. Valuable as segmenting such characteristics obviously is, no individual person can be solely defined by his or her age group, culture, or generational experience. No one segment captures the entirety of the range of a person's reactions and responses to life.

[39] Interest = promotion.

[40] Michael Lewis, "Boom Box," *The New York Times Magazine* (August 13, 2000) 65.

offend and alienate parents and authority figures but cement their target audience: anti-institutional Generation-Xers. They were willing to lose viewers from other generations in order to offer their advertisers a *pure* market segment through pristine, accurate targeting.[41] On the other hand, the preacher attempts to create community around the pluralistic task of witnessing to God's Word. The homilist's coat of arms differs dramatically from the marketer's. It reflects Psalm 133: "How good it is that brothers [and sisters] dwell together in unity."

In another way, one can see that both the marketer and homilist take advantage of the cultural and ideological differences between the generations. The marketer does so to permanently reinforce those differences. Turow agrees with this assessment of the marketer's motives:

> While media firms and advertisers used slogans such as "basic family values" and "integrity, family security, and longevity," the strategies that they adopted to profit from the various generations often served to flow with, and exploit social distance between the generations.[42]

The homilist does this as a short-term effort to draw the generations in for the long-term goal of unity. Unfortunately, the Church is divisive as well. Divisions are obvious with the current clash between neo-orthodoxy and progressive agendas, but in theory and orientation, division is not her goal.

One must remember, though, that unity cannot be sought at any cost, which is another limitation of adapting market segmentation to preaching. Preaching's ultimate purpose is not necessarily to meet people in their individual needs. The Church is called to proclaim the Good News that, paradoxically, costs us our individual preferences for a higher cause. It is a Gospel that costs us our very selves, encouraging us not only to deny ourselves but also even to die to ourselves.

The Gospel truth runs counter to our secular society's highest commandment of consumer marketing: The customer is number 1! An unreflective preoccupation with the merits of segmentation risks reducing preaching to a hollow exercise in appeasing individual, generational segments rather than inspiring collective, corporate witness. After all, the Church's goal is not simply to sell people on the benefits

[41] Turow, 106.
[42] Ibid., 69.

of individually *consuming* more of what religion offers.[43] The Gospel's ultimate goal is *producing* deeper belief and greater collective witness.

The work of Frederick Winters adds valuable insight to this discussion when he advocates a tactical segmentation. Utilizing a "decision tree"[44] methodology to illustrate his point, Winters carries market segmentation to its logical conclusion: a unique marketing mix for every individual. Obviously, this approach is not feasible or realistic for the situation of either the marketer or the preacher. The former is limited by finances and the latter by time, occasion and, most importantly, principle. Winters makes both the marketer and the preacher confront the resulting challenges:

- From either a ministerial or managerial viewpoint, what segmentation is optimal?
- At what point does segmentation become ineffective for either the purposes of the preacher or marketer?
- What is the cost-benefit payoff for the strategic goals of each?
- At what point does the tree need to be pruned to harvest the highest yield possible?

Clearly, I am advocating the subculture of generation as an optimal segmentation for the preacher, but there is a point where this segmentation becomes useless. That point is when the larger goal of building a communal connection around the truth of the Gospel becomes overshadowed by the smaller goal of individual connection that creates unity. For example, segments within Generation X could be further divided into age, socio-economic background, cultural background, education levels, then into urban or rural geographic data, or into those churched and unchurched. A further distinction of those churched is the level of their involvement. The process could go on *ad infinitum*. The possibilities of dividing are endless, but the benefits are not. Understanding how far to take the exercise of segmentation before it becomes burdensome or detrimental is the key to its effective use.

Neither the marketer nor the preacher can be all things for all people. The former will go bankrupt and the latter will lose not only the attention and believability of the congregation, but the integrity

[43] Spiritual direction, community, peace of mind, etc.

[44] Winters, 433.

of the message. If they are to maximize effectiveness, both the preacher and the marketer have to strategically decide at what point further segmentation becomes ineffective. For both, the tree needs to be pruned at the point where their final goals are not being met because the process has overshadowed or overwhelmed the product. In other words, when the medium has overtaken the message.

C. Conclusion

The author of the Christian Church's first homiletical textbook intuitively understood the multifaceted prism of cultural and generational identity as far back as the third century. St. Augustine wrote of the great difference made by an assembly's profile:

> . . . whether there are few or many; whether learned or unlearned, or a mixed audience made up of both classes; whether they are townsfolk or country folk, or both together; or a gathering in which all sorts and conditions of [humanity] are represented. For it cannot fail to be the case that different persons should affect in different ways the one who intends to instruct orally and likewise the one who intends to give formal discourse. . . .[45]

In the twenty-first century, another theologian, Generation-Xer Tom Beaudoin, illuminates the potential unifying rewards of intergenerational sensitivity as well as cautions about the divisive difficulties that accompany its failure:

> Until we have truly intergenerational teaching and learning *[and preaching]* within lay reform groups and among clergy and the hierarchy, the church will continue to have loud and soft debates. The body of Christ will stay fragmented . . . with differences allowed to fester at low temperatures.[46]

Both Augustine in his time and now Beaudoin in ours understand how critical it is to acknowledge and respect cultural and generational differences if preachers hope to build up the Body of Christ through

[45] St. Augustine quoted in Tisdale, 19.

[46] Tom Beaudoin quoted in Lefevere, 3. The addition of *[and preaching]* is mine. Appropriately, one of the last words goes to a Generation X theologian.

our "formal discourse." For our ultimate goal is not to get into the "consumer's mind so that [we] can get into his wallet"[47] but into the minds of the members of the assembly that we might get into their hearts!

If that assembly is Catholic, what precisely is the door to those multi-generational hearts arrayed before us each weekend? I propose it is the very characteristic that makes us most typically, most identifiably Catholic: our sacramental tradition. In the next chapter, we will explore the Catholic sacramental imagination as a natural and powerful threshold to effective intergenerational preaching.

[47] Lewis, 66.

The Catholic Sacramental Imagination: A Generational Bridge

5

At a doctoral presentation the candidate discussed his thesis topic, "Preaching to Children." At one point in the presentation, he displayed a slide that depicted a child's rendering of an oblong, bloated object encased by thorns. The child had explained to her teacher that this symbol was the "secret heart of Jesus," where Jesus keeps his love for us. What the child was referring to was the traditional Catholic devotion to the Sacred Heart of Jesus, whereby "his heart was to be the symbol of his divine-human love."[1]

Hearing that comment, most Catholics would chuckle at the child's innocent error and dismiss it as "cute." That instinct is unfortunate because these Catholics would miss the remarkable and deeper phenomenon of a seventeenth-century Catholic devotion being passed on to a member of our newest generation: a millennial, twenty-first-century Catholic. Particularly significant is that the knowledge of the devotion has been appropriated with its symbolic content in tact. In the child's mind she knew that God's love was the point of this devotion, that the heart was its symbol, and that the love, though real, was invisible like a secret.

After the celebration of Eucharist one day, a woman approached me about the failure of the congregation to kneel at the proper times of the Mass as decreed by the National Conference of Catholic Bishops and the local Ordinary. My answer was apparently unsatisfactory, because

[1] Leonard Foley, O.F.M., ed., *Saint of the Day,* (Cincinnati: St. Anthony Messenger Press, 1986) 274.

a week later she wrote and gave me the following quote from James Aiken's *Mass Confusion* (the bold capitals and italics are hers):

> . . . the people kneel beginning after . . . the Sanctus until after the Amens of the Eucharistic prayer, that is, before the Lord's Prayer [AGI 21]. People are **NOT** to stand up *before* the Great Amen, nor *during* it . . . it is inappropriate to be changing postures *during* this most solemn moment.
>
> In many parishes, it is also customary to kneel during the second elevation of the Host: "This is the lamb of God. . . ." Church law does not require kneelers, but it **DOES** require the *practice* of kneeling . . . **THE HOLY SEE** has ruled that the absence of kneelers is **NOT** a sufficient reason to remain standing or sitting. In fact, pastors are *required* to insure that people can *easily* assume the different postures the *liturgy* requires.[2]

She closes the letter by saying that it is a sin of disobedience to deliberately ignore the decrees of the NCCB and the local Ordinary. She points out that "even devout Muslims 'kowtow' to God five times a day kneeling on a thin prayer mat." In lieu of a signature, the letter was signed in bold capitals: "SHAME ON US."

Just as with the Millennial Catholic, it would be instinctively easy to dismiss the appreciation this Silent Generation Catholic expressed for the traditional symbolism of kneeling, albeit in a volatile tone. Rather than dismiss either of the above scenarios, it is important to study the symbolic nature of both: the generational appropriation of symbolism within the Catholic sacramental imagination. This imagination is an intricately designed box festooned with symbolic locks!

The following pages offer the keys to this sacramental lockbox by synthesizing the contributions of chapters 2 and 3 within a specifically Catholic generational milieu. Earlier, I stressed the importance of a generational exegesis of the Sunday assembly and a fuller appreciation of the influence of language and culture in the construction of generational identity. I now turn to the appropriation of these values within the context of the Catholic sacramental imagination. Specifically, this chapter will

[2] Letter from a Third Order Dominican referring to James Aiken's *Mass Confusion.*

1. Present the "hub symbol" theory articulated by theologian, Joseph Webb;[3]
2. Examine how the sacramental context of the Catholic tradition offers natural transgenerational hub symbols from which to design an intergenerational homiletic;
3. Explore areas of Catholic generational pluralism, including issues of clear generational agreement and disagreement;
4. Apply earlier insights from communications and marketing theory to a Catholic intergenerational context.

If generation is a significant and legitimate subculture that can be segmented as an important exegetical step in preaching to all age groups, understanding the process by which each group receives what is presented becomes critical. My overriding hope is to grapple with effective preaching intergenerationally in light of Catholic generational pluralism.

A. The Challenge of Pluralism

Why do we all listen to the same words when someone preaches but hear different messages? Why do we see things so differently? Why do we act so differently, and often with such emotional intensity? These are the quintessential questions, problems and challenges of pluralism from a Christian viewpoint that Joseph Webb tackles in his remarkable book. Webb traces the fascinating sojourn that the notion of pluralism has taken since its arrival on the sociological scene some forty years ago. He acknowledges that adequately defining a term as broad and complex as pluralism is a daunting challenge, especially when its conceptual understanding over the last four decades has undergone such a sea change. Let us briefly discuss the evolution of pluralism before we settle on a definition to be utilized.

In the early 1960s, pluralism referred to multiculturalism, the recognition of cultures and religions other than our own, and the concern with how to effectively preach *the* truth *to* them. The intention

[3] Joseph M. Webb, *Preaching and the Challenge of Pluralism* (St. Louis: Chalice Press, 1998) 49.

to learn about these different social and religious milieus was genuine, but the purpose was shortsighted. Like the zealous missionaries of old, we wanted to travel intellectually to these foreign cultures so as to provide "our way" and "our answers" to their inhabitants. In our minds, we were the repository of all truth, commissioned to bring that truth to others in ideologically misguided, or less benignly, heretical lands.

Twenty years later our thinking had appreciably progressed to question whether or not "converting" other cultures and religions to Christ was the point. A perspective known as *contextualism* gained strong currency reconfiguring the debate. It argued that the gospel could become indigenous to differing cultures and subcultures. The question became: "Could inculturation of the Gospel in a unique and different context offer something to our appreciation of Christianity?"

The 1990s brought the surgical strike to this debate that would fundamentally alter the landscape of the discussion. In its earlier incarnations, pluralism served to retain the vaunted place of Christianity as the indisputable center of all religious belief. Webb uses the term "new or radical pluralism" to suggest that we need to critique the uniform belief in Christianity as the end goal of pluralism. A spotlight is turned on the presumption that Christianity "has a corner on the market of correctness and truth."[4] Hence, a new and profound respect for other cultures and religions as something more than fishing territory for Christian missionaries emerges. A dialogue begins about what the unique worldviews and ideologies of these other religious traditions can teach Christianity. This growing awareness initiates a profound soul-searching and internal inquiry into the nature of a world where there is a diversity of faith traditions. Formerly considered normative, Christianity is centered as one of these. This cataclysmic shift in thinking causes an acknowledgment and, at times, painful confrontation with the raw reality of human diversity and its accompanying complications.

What is at the root of this profound diversity? Why do we see so differently? Why do we view the great issues of life from such vastly different lenses? Most importantly, how do we learn to live with and value the differences, while being true to our own beliefs? For Webb, that question is at the heart of the matter for pluralism.[5] The answer

[4] Ibid., xi.

[5] Ibid., 29.

to the dilemma lies in understanding symbol as the epicenter of all human diversity. Here I approach the concept of this new pluralism not from the traditional considerations of ethnic, racial or gender differences but from the point of view of generational diversity in religious experience and perspective.

A symbol is that which represents something else, right? Not necessarily. According to Webb, the symbolic interactionist school[6] asserts that symbol is more a means of perception than of expression.[7] It is that real or imagined vessel into which human beings innately place meaning or emotion. Thus, my earlier concept of human beings as "meaning-making machines" expands into "symbol-selecting" as well. The mind arbitrarily constructs symbols and the circumstances it selects to represent its perception. We are born with the ability to select symbols and the selection is as familiar to us as our breathing.

This discovery is breathtaking in its implications: the "real world" is more symbolic than material. The real world is not, first and foremost, what we see, feel and touch but our symbolic perception of what we see, feel and touch. We relate with each other less in the concrete than we do in the perceptual. Our cultural setting and subcultural groupings have enormous influence over the symbols we learn and appropriate. These symbols are "significant" because people invest the same meaning and emotional content as those who retain the same symbols from social or familial communities. In fact, these "significant symbols" are what provide us entry into coveted subcultures to which we want to belong. The key to this process is that no symbol, however common, contains an objective universal significance. People never affix the same cognitive or emotional content to a symbol because no two individuals focus on a person, place or object in the same way. This occurs all the time as, for example, when a friend

[6] Ibid., 47. This tradition comes from the Chicago School of Sociology at the turn of the twentieth century. It represents the principle theory of pluralism that lies at the foundation of Webb's work. Symbolic interactionism explores human interaction at the interpersonal and collective levels through the lens of language, human relationship and action, personal and global confrontation and the dynamics of preaching. Within this tradition, "lies a profound viewpoint on the volatility of human behavior, one that gives us some unique insights into the question of why we treat so badly people who think and act differently than we do." It has clear and deep connections to our understanding of human symbolism and is fundamental to the nature of being human.

[7] Webb, 17.

accompanies us to a new place with strangers. While given the same information and privy to the same interaction, people usually walk away with different impressions.

These two dimensions of symbol, cognitive and emotional, form what are known as symbol systems. Language is the most commonly understood example of such a system, although not the underlying or fundamental ingredient of human communication. Others would include action, ritual, gesture, space and sexuality.[8] Therein lies the crux of symbol selecting: anything and anyone is potential fodder for human symbol making. Which symbolic meaning arbitrarily bestowed on an event, person or thing is the true one? Yours or mine? If we cannot agree on that issue, how can we frame a common dialogue respectful of each other's differences about values, norms and attitudes? Why do such concerns so often presage a societal and cultural minefield rather than an opportunity to celebrate the richness of diversity? The answer to this question and all that has been discussed above culminates in Webb's theory of *hub symbols*.

B. Hub Symbols: Pluralism Made Concrete

Hub symbols are the organizing principles around which human symbol selecting and constructing coalesce. Webb uses the image of a well to describe the depth of emotional intensity with which we form our symbolic perspectives of people, things and events. From these perspectives, we unconsciously organize and arrange an all-encompassing worldview. We imbue this intuitive symbol-arranging process with a sacredness that defies rationality. Thus, we unconsciously create hub symbols that we regard as ultimate and inviolate, even "holy." It is not difficult, then, to understand how quickly our differences become occasions for irrational hostility. This sociological phenomenon is at the core of all conflict regardless of the issue or its emotional intensity.

Metaphorically, hub symbols take their name from the hub of a wheel. The deeper "the well of emotion" reflected in a symbol, the closer that symbol is to the hub of the wheel. The reverse is also true. What is important to remember is that attacking a person's hub symbols is akin to a perceived act of violence against that person. When we threaten hub symbols, we threaten ultimate ways of seeing the

[8] Ibid., 17.

world and seeing ourselves. It is an assault against all the tiny threads that represent the values holding our symbolic universes together. The woman who was very upset over the lack of kneeling during the Eucharist provides a case in point. Her intense reaction was provoked by a perceived threat to her hub symbol of not simply liturgical reverence but of actual belief.

Our web of interconnected hub symbols becomes "the real world" in which we live daily. Those at the very center of our world are the most likely to produce the most intense reaction, usually leading to confrontation. Tragically, the most familiar and immediately relevant examples of this tension are the religious conflicts still plaguing the Middle East, Northern Ireland, and the continuing tension between Western Christianity and radical Islam.

Implications for Intergenerational Preachers

Intergenerational preachers deal in a world of symbols. They are less the proverbial wordsmith, but more a "symbolsmith" who, in performing their artistry, surf the net of interlocking symbol systems and alight for a time on the dock of individual symbolic universes. In order to competently blend these symbolic galaxies (echoes of Fern Johnson and communicative competence),[9] preachers must understand the basic hub symbols of each generation. They need to recognize that consideration of each generation's symbolic mix[10] is inherent in the intergenerational preaching process of creating the right marketing mix. Just as the marketing mix is a creative manipulation of the four Ps *(product, price, placement* and *promotion),* the symbolic mix is an ongoing, creative process of organizing and redefining previous and current symbolic material. As Webb explains:

> One draws on one's past symbols, gives them a twist of unique meaning, boils some unique emotion into them, merges them with other already charged symbols, from past or present, and then acts on the basis of that symbolic "summing up". . . . Every individual who assimilates a definition must, in turn, reframe that definition or bit of information within his or her own previous symbolic mix.[11]

[9] See Johnson, 30.
[10] Webb, 36.
[11] Ibid., 36.

What Webb describes above as an individual phenomenon also occurs generationally. Let us explore a more profound application of Webb's hub symbol theory within the Catholic sacramental imagination.

The Eucharist is the preeminent hub symbol that is "ultimate and inviolate" within the Catholic sacramental tradition. It is the quintessential symbol system that is a part of each generation's symbolic mix and around which the whole Catholic symbolic universe coalesces. The cognitive and emotional dimensions of this liturgical, sacramental, theological, and deeply spiritual hub symbol are intergenerational as well as truly transgenerational. The depth of emotional upset felt by the Mass attendee when the assembly did not kneel during the Eucharistic Prayer is an accurate indicator of its close placement at the very hub of Catholicism's sacramental life. The following example illustrates this phenomenon from another perspective that highlights the generational reframing and creative re-appropriation of this sacred hub symbol.

The College Church on the campus of Saint Louis University invites parishioners to Eucharist Adoration every Friday at noon. On the same campus Adoration of the Blessed Sacrament also occurs on Monday nights at ten o'clock in the Notre Dame Residence Hall. Exposition of the Blessed Sacrament was believed to be an ocular moment of communion, which brings grace to the soul, allowing those present to be nourished by Christ without actually receiving the body and blood of Jesus. It is the same Eucharistic ritual event, expressive of the same core belief in the Real Presence,[12] but dramatically different in celebratory tone and generational participation.

A person attending the College Church ritual would recognize the traditional Catholic approach to Eucharistic Adoration practiced with few modifications since the seventeenth century: a silent, contemplative, and private act of personal piety before a raised mon-

[12] The Real Presence refers to the Catholic belief in transubstantiation which the *Catechism of the Catholic Church* defines as "the body and blood, together with the soul and divinity, of Our Lord Jesus Christ and, therefore, *the whole Christ is truly, really, and substantially* contained. This presence is called 'real' by which is not intended to exclude the other types of presence as if they could not be 'real' too, but because it is presence in the fullest sense: that is to say, it is a *substantial* presence by which Christ, God and man, makes himself wholly and entirely present." *Catechism of the Catholic Church,* no. 1373 (Washington, D.C.: United States Catholic Conference, 1994) 346.

strance containing the Blessed Sacrament. One's posture would be a quiet, reverential awe and awareness of the Transcendent. A church environment of hushed silence, penitential posture and the unmistakable scent of billowing clouds of incense would help this ambience. The generations most commonly seen in the pews are the "Silent and Builders" (those approximately sixty and over), often praying the rosary, with a smattering of Baby Boomers (those age thirty-six to fifty-nine).

A person attending the Monday night ritual would encounter a population overwhelmingly representative of Generation X with a clear and creative reinterpretation of the traditional ritual just described. While the Eucharist is reverently exposed on the altar in a monstrance, the atmosphere is festive with the tone of a revival. There is a scriptural reading followed by a brief testimonial and then an alternating Taizé-like[13] rhythmic chanting with contemporary praise, intercession and lively song. The most profound difference is the lack of silence with the traditional contemplative posture of distant awe before the Blessed Sacrament. The emphasis is on active and affective involvement with bodily gestures, verbal prayer, and vocal praise. Yet, the Monday night ritual is no less reverent than its more traditional counterpoint but simply reflects a redefinition of reverence.

This redefinition reflects its generation's desire for an immanent, more tangible, touchable, up-close Jesus. This generation's Jesus is not solely transcendent. Rather than sitting in pews, the young people are sprawled out on the floor underneath the monstrance, some sitting, some standing, and some kneeling directly in front of the Blessed Sacrament. About fifty to fifty-five college students pack the small chapel with about fifteen religious. The event is usually led by a young Jesuit seminarian and a twenty-something sister from the Daughters of St. Paul.

Their message and presentation is solidly Catholic, maybe, by some interpretations, even neo-orthodox. But their style is "down-home and personal," and very charismatic. What was traditionally a private, meditative moment is transformed into a public, informal, active, communal event. Whatever the interpretation, it clearly reflects the symbolic summarizing posited by Joseph Webb. While the

[13] Taizé Prayer originated in a French ecumenical community primarily known for its mantra form of musical participation.

overall symbolic meaning and emotional content of the "Generation X Eucharistic Adoration" is the same as the original, more traditional ritual, the differences in style reflect one generation's drawing on a past generation's symbolic devotion and giving it Webb's "twist." In doing so, the Gen-Xers drew from their personal and generational symbolic mix and redefined it "with full meaning and emotion reconfigured, but still intact."[14] Therefore, preachers need to draw upon this rich symbolic tradition, recognize this phenomenon of retrieval and re-appropriation and listen for each generation's contribution to the tradition's ongoing reinterpretation and revivification. Specifically, they must carefully consider author Robert Weber's observation that for younger generations in our current culture, unlike the "heady days" of the Enlightenment,

> Information is no longer something that can be objectively known and verified through evidence and logic. Knowledge is more subjective and experiential. Knowledge comes through participation in a community and in an immersion with the symbols and meaning of that community.[15]

To appreciate better the above scenarios of Eucharistic Adoration, both in their similarities and differences, it is important to recognize that to be Catholic is to be steeped in sign, symbol and the power of ritual. Powerful symbol systems operate within Catholic sacramental communication and liturgical ritual. Therefore, it is crucial to grasp fully the Catholic sacramental system before further discussion of its relevance to intergenerational preaching. We will examine this tradition from scholastic (St. Thomas Aquinas, O.P.) and contemporary theological (Mary Catherine Hilkert, O.P.) viewpoints.

C. The Catholic Sacramental Tradition

In order to understand Aquinas, we must examine St. Augustine who greatly influenced Thomas. The writings of Augustine reveal his understanding that sacraments are visible signs of the invisible mystery of Christ actively sanctifying his Church through the grace they confer. For Augustine, sacraments always comprise two elements:

[14] Webb, 37.

[15] Robert Weber quoted in Roberto, 3.

"a sign *(signum)* and some sacred thing *(res)*."[16] The Latin word *sacramentum* from which the English word "sacrament" is derived has a much broader reality to Augustine than the Church's seven sacraments. According to the *Catechism of the Catholic Church, sacramentum* is a translation of the Greek word *mysterion* ("mystery") and describes

> the visible sign of the hidden reality of salvation. . . . In this sense, Christ himself is the mystery of salvation. . . . The saving work of his [Christ's] holy and sanctifying humanity is the sacrament of salvation, which is revealed and active in the Church's sacraments.[17]

For Augustine, this sacred sign, this *sacramentum,* can be anything that "shows forth, indeed brings about, what is not in the physical sense able to be seen"[18] and thus has the quality of divine revelation. So the visible, perceptible property of sign with its veiled reality of grace plays a critical part in Augustine's thinking and is the foundation of the thought of Thomas Aquinas.

St. Thomas begins the sacramental tract of the *Summa Theologiae* by quoting Augustine's *City of God.*[19] Aquinas leaves no doubt about the primary importance Augustine plays in his thinking. For Aquinas, "God shows us in the sacraments what he [God] does and does what he [God] shows."[20] David Bourke explains:

> If there is one idea, which lies at the very roots of St. Thomas's treatise as a whole, it is the idea that the new life of the redemption wrought by God in the Incarnate Word is communicated to man [humanity] through created media, physical things, or acts combined by words.[21]

This phenomenon is further illustrated through our opening example of the Eucharist as a transgenerational symbol through which God most perfectly communicates God's self. Aquinas appreciates the power of the Eucharist in precisely this way. If the sacraments are

[16] Brian Davies, *The Thought of Thomas Aquinas* (London: Oxford University Press, 1992) 347.

[17] *Catechism of the Catholic Church,* 205.

[18] Davies, 347.

[19] Ibid., 349. "The visible sacrifice is the sacrament, i.e., the sacred sign, of the invisible sacrifice."

[20] Davies, 351.

[21] Ibid., 350.

human realities through which the invisible God comes to us, the "physical things" of bread and wine are the outward signs *par excellence* of God's self-communication. For Thomas the six other sacraments are oriented toward the Eucharist,[22] which he asserts, "constitutes the goal and consummation of all the sacraments."[23]

From Catholic, Thomistic points of view, the sacraments are physical human signs that go beyond mere symbol because they effect a graced transformation that heals and makes whole. Thomas explains, "Just as the physical body of Jesus has given us the invisible God, the physical signs that are the sacraments truly give us the healing love of the invisible God."[24] This explanation highlights why, for many Catholics across generations, the Eucharist is such an emotionally charged hub symbol. For whatever their other issues of agreement or disagreement with the Church,[25] the Eucharist is the source of that healing power spoken of by Aquinas for their spiritual and sacramental lives. In the final analysis, the most significant hub symbol for the Catholic is that "outward sign of the Eucharist, bread and wine eaten [which] signifies the intimate union of Jesus in the depths of our being."[26] Under the disguise of symbolic physical elements is a reality beyond the symbols. As Richard Conrad, O.P., notes, "Jesus is at work in them so that through them we are drawn to God and made receptive to further gifts."[27]

Echoing both Augustine and Aquinas' broader sense of sacrament and its dual revelatory character, Dominican Gerald Vann offers an applicable example:

> We say sacrament is an outward sign of an inward grace. We are familiar with outward signs of inward states or experiences: the heightened color, for instance, that shows joy or anger or excitement; and a sacrament is something visible like that, but it shows a divine activity going on within the soul, the touch of God's hand.[28]

[22] Mary Ann Fatula, O.P., *Thomas Aquinas: Preacher and Friend* (Collegeville: The Liturgical Press, 1993) 253.

[23] Davies, 367.

[24] Fatula, 251.

[25] This specific issue will be discussed later.

[26] Fatula, 258.

[27] Richard Conrad, O.P., *The Catholic Faith: A Dominican's Vision* (New York: Geoffrey Chapman, 1994) 6.

[28] Gerald Vann, O.P., *The Pain of Christ and the Sorrow of God* (New York: Alba House, 1947) 4.

The contributions to this discussion of two other influential teachers of sacraments between Augustine and Aquinas, Hugh of St. Victor and Peter Lombard, bear mention at this point. According to Aquinas scholar Brian Davies, Hugh of St. Victor made a significant and lasting impact with his definition of *sacramentum*.[29] Lombard develops Hugh of St. Victor's notion of spiritual grace by making the important assertion that grace has a clear causal effect.[30] Aquinas will embrace this understanding as well as Lombard's precise emphasis on what has become the official church doctrine of strictly seven sacraments. While secondary to the dominant place of Augustine in Aquinas' sacramental thinking, the influences of St. Hugh of Victor and Peter Lombard were crucial, historical complements.

In contemporary theology, Sr. Mary Catherine Hilkert, O.P., has made an important contribution to this concept. Drawing on the theology of Karl Rahner, she asserts that preaching in a postmodern world requires embracing a sacramental vision of reality that *names grace* as a gift here and now within the guise of everyday life. "Naming grace" identifies and locates the sacramental presence—the invisible within the visible—of God and the concrete reality of the Gospel within contemporary human experience and the Christian community of believers.

The essence of her thought is this: in the midst of the brokenness of the human condition through the reality of sin, the grace of God is manifest, operative, and ultimately more powerful than either sin or its symptoms. She not only acknowledges the valid concerns of Karl Barth's dialectical imagination but also exhorts a critical engagement with its tenets. Hilkert affirms the sacramental power of the incarnation as the more decisive reality. "If preachers are to point to God's continued action in human history, the incarnational principle remains central: God is active in and through humankind."[31] Yet Hilkert warns that the sacramental fulfillment of God's initiative requires the community of believers to witness to its promise. She speaks of Jesus as "the primary sacrament of God's presence among us—the making

[29] Davies, 348. "A sacrament is a physical or material element admitted to the perception of the eternal senses, representing a reality beyond itself in virtue of having been instituted as a sign of it and containing within itself some invisible and spiritual grace in virtue of having been consecrated."

[30] Ibid., 348.

[31] Mary Catherine Hilkert, O.P., *Naming Grace* (New York: Continuum, 1998) 193.

visible of the invisible God."[32] In that light, "the church, living communities of the baptized, are called to continue to bear witness to the mystery that 'compassion is at the heart of reality' . . . [and] the sacramental imagination asserts, . . . sacraments 'effect what they signify.'"[33]

Hilkert represents a Catholic woman's viewpoint that builds on the sacramental understanding of grace as always present within humanity. Grace is the source and effect of genuine human transformation. Human sin, while damaging, is never able to completely corrupt the created goodness of humanity.[34]

Hilkert's departure point is Rahner's premise that "all reality is structured symbolically—signs of grace are to be found everywhere one has 'eyes to see.'"[35] God's presence is continually mediated in human history through these signs of grace. The invitation to divine friendship is constantly extended through the manifestation of grace in the concrete reality of our everyday words and actions. Hilkert concurs with Rahner that there is never a moment when human beings stand outside the invitation to God's friendship, outside the possibility of grace. Within the Church, grace is found in the proclamation of the Word and the celebration of the sacraments. Is this not Augustine's "visible words" that bring grace, the depth dimension of reality to recognition and thus effective power?[36] Again we are back to Hilkert's assertion that words are graced. They are *depth words* that in the case of the preacher or community of believers, "effect what they signify."[37] She demonstrates the influence of Augustine in her own thought as she reminds us of his insight: "sacraments are visible words; words are audible sacraments."[38] In her way of thinking, preaching is always a profound liturgical and sacramental act that audibly names the hidden grace present and active in visible history and daily life.

By their very nature, the sacraments build up the Church, which in herself is a sacramental sign and instrument,[39] through the mediation of God's presence in polyvalent symbol and ritual. Through the rich

[32] Hilkert, 190.
[33] Ibid., 190.
[34] Ibid., 46.
[35] Rahner, quoted in Hilkert, 32.
[36] Hilkert, 47.
[37] Ibid., 190.
[38] Ibid., 192.
[39] *Catechism of the Catholic Church*, no. 775, 204.

complex of Catholic sacramental life, the Church continues to reveal herself as "the visible plan of God's love for humanity."[40] Conrad captures this reality best: "It is in the continuity of her historical identity, in her visible unity, in her infallible teaching of the faith, in her liturgy and especially in the sacraments, that the Church is herself sacramental."[41]

Church life and worship is expressed in visible and sacramental forms. Catholic liturgical signs and symbols are analogous to generational signs and symbols. Intergenerational preaching is effective if it intuitively appreciates the polyvalent nature of the Catholic sacramental tradition. There is a natural marriage between the innately sacramental view of Roman Catholicism and intergenerational preaching, for the latter appreciates the power of sign and symbol, which is such an inherent part of the former. This appreciation is born out of an understanding of the nonlinear, image-driven, empirical approaches to learning that changed from earlier generations' emphasis on memorized facts in a linear progression toward truth. Thus, intergenerational preaching is a natural, cultural and linguistic bridge between generational hub symbols that honor sacramental reality and generational experience, both of which, although different, communicate in a realm beyond our sense experience.

Intergenerational preaching, rooted in the Catholic sacramental imagination, has the potential to reconcile religious generational divisions. It reemphasizes how we know God, each other and ourselves in the collective sacramental symbols we share as Church. Such preaching respects and does not negate the symbol systems of each particular generation. Nathan Mitchell describes how sacraments launch a truthful search and a process of discovery "through which we reconnect with something absent, something missing, something unknown, something, in short, *transcendent*."[42] The great paradox of symbols is that they "call us to the threshold of *presence* by first leading us through an abyss of *absence*."[43] Thus, the goal of intergenerational preaching is to collectively lead varied generations, each having their individual symbol systems, through that *absence* to the threshold of *presence*. As we have seen with the prime Catholic hub symbol of the

[40] Paul VI, discourse of June 22, 1973.
[41] Conrad, 195.
[42] Nathan Mitchell, quoted in Hilkert, 192.
[43] Hilkert, 192.

Eucharist, we must bridge those symbol systems at their "generational hubs" of faith consensus and shared belief. This will lead us to the more concrete issue of specific generational agreement/disagreement with regard to the hub symbols of faith and morality.

D. Catholic Generational Agreement and Disagreement

Joseph Webb's hub symbol theory and the contributions of Aquinas and Hilkert to our understanding of the Catholic sacramental tradition naturally lead us to an exploration of the formative years from a Catholic generational perspective. What is the process by which a particular perspective becomes normative for an age group? What makes it a "cohort"? To answer these questions we turn to Karl Mannheim, the "Father of Generation Theory" and an interpreter of his theory, Walrath.[44]

Mannheim was the first to study generational variation in the early 1950s, arguing that long-term attitudes and behaviors are decisively formed in adolescence. People born during one time period share a specific worldview and vision that is vastly different than those born in another period. This is due to collective exposure to similar geographic, societal, and historic phenomena, the convergence of which creates a united worldview. Therefore, "persons belonging to a particular generation, or birth cohort, have a shared vision of the world."[45]

Applying Mannheim's theory, Walrath suggests that what we experience socially, politically, economically and religiously in our formative years (ages 13 to 22) has a lasting impact on our lifelong behavior and attitudes. These historic and cultural experiences become the unique framework out of which they develop their worldview and by which they continue to define future experiences. This explains why people can go through similar life stages and experiences but have qualitatively different understandings of what those experiences mean. While in the course of life, all generations embark

[44] James D. Davidson, Andrea S. Williams, Richard A. Lamanna, Jan Stenftenagel, Kathleen Maas Weigert, William J. Whalen, Patricia Wittberg, S.C., *The Search for Common Ground: What Unites and Divides Catholic Americans* (Huntington, Ind.: Our Sunday Visitor, 1997) 112.

[45] Davidson, 112.

chronologically upon similar experiences, they perceive them in dramatically different ways and "never let go of the experienced differences."[46] Those younger, who are socialized at a different historical time than their elders, do not take on the perspectives of previous generations but "hang on" to their own formative learning experiences. This is what makes them a cohort.

In order to fully appreciate the similarities and dissimilarities between Catholic generational cohorts and how the various age groups agree and disagree from a generational perspective, we need to utilize the marketer's segmentation tool and be mindful of our earlier discussion of culture, language, and meaning.

If "history creates generations and generations create history,"[47] what are the historically social and religious influences that have shaped generations of Catholics? In what "Catholic Church" were they formed? Utilizing the same schema for segmenting Catholic generational cohorts as John Roberto and Ronald Allen employed for secular generational constellations gives us a snapshot of Catholic generational perspective and identity. Specifically, this segmentation offers insight into the formative cultural and religious influences predominant in the years before, during, and after the most tumultuous historical period in the Church this century, the Second Vatican Council.

Since its closing session in December 1965, the Council has been a lightening rod between enthusiasts and apologists on both sides of the ideological spectrum. Wherever one finds him/herself on this continuum, the depth of feeling the Council still evokes today is a testament to the intensity of its perceived threat or great hope. From either perspective, its actions were seen as groundbreaking and precedent-shattering. Whether good or bad, a new springtime or a deadly winter, most agreed the Council had ushered in a new era in the Church. Dean Hoge, professor of sociology at The Catholic University of America, captures the breathtaking steps envisioned and formulated by the Council:

> The Council affirmed the ecumenical movement, endorsed religious freedom of conscience in all nations, and expressed openness and some optimism regarding modern secular systems of thought. The Council also mandated liturgical innovation, encouraged the

[46] Davidson, 113.

[47] Neil Howe and William Strauss, *The Fourth Turning: An American Prophecy* (New York: Broadway Books, 1997) 16.

> religious orders to update themselves and their missions in the context of modern society, and asked for the establishment of decision-making procedures involving broader participation—including senates of priests in each diocese and parish councils in each parish.[48]

In their groundbreaking, seminal work *The Search for Common Ground,* James Davidson and his associates of Purdue University try to show how Catholics growing up after Vatican II differ from those who came of age during and before the Council. They categorize Catholics into three distinct generational cohorts: those raised in the Pre-Vatican II Church, during Vatican II and Post-Vatican II. Table 2, depicting the key societal and Catholic influences formative of each generation, was created and organized drawing heavily, although not exclusively, from their work.[49]

What insights can be drawn from this chart? Clearly, according to Davidson, our three cohorts were formed in very different societal, cultural and Catholic milieus. While age is a factor in these differences, more significant is that these differences represent the varied experiences of generations during their formative years.[50] Specifically, the definitive realities for the oldest cohort were the Great Depression and World War II, while for the middle cohort the formative influences were affluent, post-war America and the cultural, social, and sexual revolutions of the 1960s. The youngest cohort experienced the economic disparity and daunting cultural challenges of the last two decades.[51] These generations were raised in three strikingly different Catholic environments. Thus, their experience of Catholicism varies dramatically. This fact accounts for not only an alternate religious approach but also a faith perspective whose departure point will always be the learning in these crucial formative years.

[48] Dean Hoge, *Converts, Dropouts, Returnees: A Study of Religious Change among Catholics* (New York: The Pilgrim Press, 1981) 22.

[49] This chart was created and organized by drawing upon the following sources: Davidson; Rick and Kathy Hicks, *Boomers, Xers, and Other Strangers: Understanding the Generational Differences That Divide Us* (Wheaton, Ill.: Tyndale House, 1999); William Strauss and Neil Howe, *Millennials Rising: The Next Great Generation* (New York: Vintage Books, 2000); Tom Beaudoin, *Virtual Faith* (San Francisco: Jossey-Bass, 1998); Robert A. Ludwig, *Reconstructing Catholicism for a New Generation* (New York: Crossroad, 1996).

[50] Davidson, 203.

[51] Ibid., 203.

Table 2: Catholic Generational Cohorts with Key Cultural and Catholic Influences

Catholic Generations	Key Cultural Influences	Key Catholic Influences
Pre-Vatican II Church Formed: 1920s, 30s, 40s	Prosperity of Roaring 20s Depression: Economic hardship WWII: Evils of Nazism Help from families and government Authority conscious Sought peace and common good Prohibition Government involvement/ The New Deal	Immigrant communities Blue collar/working class Traditional symbols Networking organizations "Ghetto mentality" Stressed church practice Doctrinal uniformity Institutional model
Vatican II Church Formed: 1950s, 60s	Tranquility of Eisenhower years Radical social movements of 60s Respected/Questioned authority Civil Rights Movement Vietnam War Protests Institutions to individualism Political assassinations Korea to Cuba/Cold War	Foot in "old/new" church Baltimore *Catechism*/Vatican II World now "positive" Ecumenism/truth expands Guide: Church to conscience Greater lay involvement Classical to historic consciousness Collegial model
Post-Vatican II Church Formed: 1970s, 80s	Prosperity of Roaring 90s Decrease in discrimination Increase: Women's opportunities Increase: Environmental concerns Watergate/Whitewater 3-mile Island/Chernobyl Challenger tragedy Fear of AIDS Increased divorce among parents Vietnam to Iran No middle class High unemployment Huge income gap Distrust authorities Religion as social institution	Virtual ministry/cyberspace Experiential approach to faith Guitar Masses Individualistic faith journey "Deconstructed Context" Decrease: Ritual/obedience Revival of mysticism "Sacramental" in pop culture More Christian than Catholic Favor social justice Multiple expressions of *Catholic* Campus Newman Centers Desire democratic model

Davidson maintains that these generational variations also signal diminished "'childhood religiosity,' closeness to God, and commitment to the Church."[52] Post-Vatican II Catholics are not as institutionally religious in their youth as older generations were in theirs. They do not readily sense experiences of God's daily presence and their institutional commitment is significantly weaker.[53] He warns that these trends not only indicate a continuing erosion of Catholic identity and church credibility but also reflect the growing propensity to disagree with traditional church positions on faith and morals while embracing contrary beliefs and ideas.

These varied cultural and religious influences bear a direct correlation to generational differences in faith and morals. This is the essence of Davidson's conclusion: generational birth cohorts provide the most trustworthy key to predicting one's perspective on faith and morals. Further segmenting allows us to study the specific generational differences regarding the myriad of issues dealing with faith and morality.

Research by Dean Hoge builds upon Davidson and his team's work. Hoge tackles generational agreement and disagreement, offering a valuable vista by which to view the concrete application of Davidson's thinking. Coupling Davidson's insights with the work of a research group at The Catholic University of America (CU), Hoge focuses on age variations regarding opinions on topics of faith and morals. Utilizing multiple national surveys of Catholics in six age groups representing Davidson's generational cohorts, the CU research group compiled data on the age differences in church attitudes and religious behavior. Table 3 organizes this work concerning church positions on faith and morals according to the categories: *largest*, *moderately large* or *none.*[54]

Hoge's research reveals several noteworthy tendencies: (1) The older generations focus on devotion and responsible practice of their faith, while the younger ones are more concerned with inclusivity and democratic participation. (2) The older generations believe strongly

[52] Ibid., 204. The term "childhood religiosity" refers to "the extent to which youngsters are subjectively and behaviorally involved in the Church."

[53] Davidson, 204.

[54] Dean R. Hoge, "Catholic Generational Differences: Can we learn anything by identifying the specific issues of generational agreement and disagreement?" *America* (October 2, 1999) 14–17.

Table 3: Catholic Generational Cohorts' Issues

Catholic Generations	Issues among All Three Generations	Differences
Pre-Vatican II Formative Years 1930s, 1940s born before 1940 **Vatican II** Formative Years 1950s, 1960s born 1940–1960 **Post-Vatican II** Formative Years 1970s, 1980s born after 1960	**Sexual Morality** Pre-marital sex,* birth control, homosexual acts Reception of communion for divorce Catholics without annulment **Mass Attendance and Devotions** Daily Eucharist, rosary Devotions to Mary and the saints **Attitudes toward Lay Leaders** **Attitudes about Women's Roles**	**Largest:** *All disagree* Older says: "Always wrong" Young say: "It all depends" (*topic with most polarization) Older Catholics do much more of all these Young advocate more in choosing parish priests and formulating church teachings on birth control Disagree that women's primary role is care of home and support of husband's career
Same	**Whether:** Abortion can be a moral choice? Divorces should be easier to obtain? Priests should be allowed to marry? Bishops should consult laity on sexual issues? Catholics should obey pope over conscience? Respondent could be as happy in other church?	**Moderately Large** *Some disagreement, but small*
Same	**Eucharist** **Life after Death** **Desirability of more Democracy** **Greater Lay Involvement** **More Church Roles for Women** **Evaluation of Parishes** **Capital Punishment**	**None:** *All Agree* Bread and wine are actually transformed into Body and Blood of Christ At the levels of parish, diocese, and the Vatican In decisions about money, church documents on economic justice and world peace Specifically: lectors, eucharistic ministers, altar servers, deacons Welcoming? Spirituality helpful? Meet needs? Opposition

in moral absolutes especially regarding sexual issues. The young believe that moral situations and choices are not always "cut and dry," requiring one to remain open to the unique circumstances of the scenario. (3) The critical chasm in generational differences is not between Pre-Vatican II and Post-Vatican II but between Pre-Vatican II and Vatican II.

According to Hoge, the razor edge of age differences is found at approximately age fifty. (4) All generations agree on the core teachings of the Catholic Church that form the heart of the faith while the largest generational differences are over peripheral issues. (5) The young are not alienated from their faith but are drawn to the Church by the same spiritual hungers that have been driving their predecessors over the last millennium. However, it is the dramatic social, political, and sexual movements of the 1960s that are most directly responsible for the greatest generational differences. Hoge concludes on an optimistic note that these generational differences need not alarm us. Rather, they serve as encouragement for the old to reach out to the young.[55]

E. Conclusion

Hoge and Davidson both help clarify how different Catholic generations stand in relation to one another and to the Church. The greatest unity of all age groups lies in core Catholic beliefs and practices. While there is a definite movement away from conventual faith practices and moral absolutes among the Post-Vatican II segment, generational variations are minor in the essential teachings of the Church. This finding provides a viable basis for intergenerational preaching within a Catholic sacramental context.

The next chapter provides a "test-case" for intergenerational preaching, encompassing all of our learning to this point.

[55] Ibid., 14–17.

Does It Work? The Mechanics of Intergenerational Preaching

6

When I contacted one of the three parishes selected as a possible intergenerational preaching site, the associate pastor relayed to me the initial reaction of his pastor: "Intergenerational preaching? What's novel about that? We do that here every Sunday." The pastor's reaction is telling. He believes that they are preaching intergenerationally because their Sunday assembly is an intergenerational gathering. This is precisely the faulty assumption that I have sought to expose and mend. Before proceeding, a summary of the foundation laid earlier in this work offers a helpful retrospective.

We first explored the role that culture, language, and communication play in the construction of generations. Then we proposed that an effective and life-giving word preached to different generations in the same setting requires knowledge of these groups' cultural self-references, linguistic habits, and their meaning within respective generational cohorts. Since preaching is a speech act, effective discourse depends upon not only knowing *what* generation one is attempting to reach but also *how* to reach it. Therefore, a clear knowledge of each generation's unique lexicon of words, metaphors and phraseology is essential. For the purposes of this study, those generations were described as: Builders, *The Institutional Generation* (1901–1924); The Silent Generation, *Bridge Builders* (1925–1942); Baby Boomers, *Visionaries and Seekers* (1943–1961/64); Generation-X, *A Relational Generation* (1961/64–1981);[1] The Millennial Generation, *Young Navigators* (1981–present).[2]

[1] Allen, 369–400.

[2] Roberto, 1.

In Chapter 2, we analyzed the "crisis" of preaching from both Catholic and Protestant perspectives. While not suggesting multiple ways to meet this crisis, the study highlighted the rich possibilities of intergenerational preaching to reenergize the field of homiletics. Intergenerational preaching was defined as "preaching the gospel message in a culturally relevant and life-giving manner to the arguably four to five generations comprising the Sunday assembly."

Chapter 3 argued that generation is a subculture akin to ethnicity, race, and gender. We discussed a *generational segmentation* of one's congregation through the application of contemporary market segmentation practices. These strategies were adapted to preaching, delineating both market segmentation's contributions and limitations. The thesis of this book claimed that: "intergenerational preaching represents a homiletic approach that embraces a qualified segmentation based on the subculture of generation." This led to the assertion that multiple generations can and must be reached simultaneously. Thus exegeting one's congregation generationally must be a serious step in homiletic preparation.

Finally, Chapter 4 explored generational pluralism. Insights from this exploration were applied to a Catholic intergenerational context by examining how the Roman Catholic sacramental tradition forms a natural trans-generational "hub symbol" from which to design an intergenerational homiletic. The Eucharist served as a primary example.

This chapter will explain the preparation, execution and feedback of the preaching event that tested my hypothesis: "one can preach to all generations in the same setting by invoking generation-specific references." Specifically, five steps were followed:

A. Description: understanding of sites chosen for the project

B. Methodology: approach for obtaining data

C. Examination: how the homiletical approach was used to target the five generations

D. Analysis: written and oral

   1. Collating the written evaluations from parishioners who represented all generations

   2. Summarizing the verbal feedback from all focus groups designed with Pre-Vatican II, Vatican II and Post-Vatican II cohorts

E. Drawing conclusions: what the data tells us regarding the thesis statement

A. Description of Intergenerational Preaching Sites

Three local parishes were selected as sites to test my intergenerational preaching hypothesis:

- 5:00 P.M. Saturday evening Eucharist at St. Jerome in Troy, Ill.
- 9:00 A.M. Sunday Eucharist at St. Peter in Kirkwood, Mo.
- 11:00 A.M. Sunday celebration of Eucharist at Washington University, St. Louis.

St. Jerome Catholic Church is located in Troy, Illinois, in the Springfield Diocese. This mid-state Illinois parish draws approximately five hundred families from a broad geographic area. It is a predominantly white, middle-class, closely-knit "bedroom community" of St. Louis, Missouri. The church grows approximately fifty families a year.

St. Jerome is a small community that offers a contemporary/classical approach to its music. The parish has a reputation for dynamic preaching and a strong spirit of hospitality. It also emphasizes lay involvement with a variety of special ministries for all age groups. Service to others is a strong parish value particularly evident in its ministry to the East St. Louis, Illinois, poor and St. Jerome parish elderly shut-ins.

The second site chosen was St. Peter in Kirkwood, a near suburb of St. Louis. It is predominantly middle to upper income, with a population of approximately one thousand Anglo families of European descent (only 5 percent are African American). St. Peter is another very active, dynamic parish that encourages lay involvement. A strong proponent of continuing religious education, the parish is host to local Bible study and faith sharing groups offering formation for both children and adults. It also has a strong liturgy and music program, while boasting the largest number of parishioners involved in the archdiocesan *Renew* program.

St. Peter is unique among my three choices because of its strong political leanings toward the conservative due to the large number of state representatives and senators registered in the parish. The 9:00 A.M. Eucharist was attended by about 50 percent family-age adults with very small children and 50 percent older adults. Teenagers were the least represented group.

The Catholic Student Center at Washington University was my final site. While its Newman Community is primarily a college-age ministry, its 11:00 A.M. Eucharist draws other generations from the surrounding neighborhood as well as the families of graduate students, alumni, staff and faculty. Built to be more of a small campus chapel than a full-fledged parish church, the space is friendly and intimate. The first pew is not more than a yard from the sanctuary!

This Newman Community, worshiping in an academic environment, is an unusually well-educated assembly. The whole congregation, including a 50 percent student population, is multicultural but predominantly Euro-American. In terms of socioeconomic status, it shares more in common with St. Peter than with St. Jerome by being predominantly, but not exclusively, middle to upper class. The Catholic Center's well-prepared liturgies and preachings consistently draw out-of-town congregants.

All three parishes were chosen for three reasons. Each would:

- Reflect a broad homogeneous character
- Provide the research control element of a balanced intergenerational assembly encompassing the five generations studied
- Insure the full cooperation of the parish leadership in the project "test case"

B. Methodology

I used the following means to test the effectiveness of my intergenerational method:

- A feedback form distributed to each member of the assembly (see Appendix 1)
- Oral data gathered from focus groups representing all three Catholic Generational Cohorts would be gathered after the Eucharist

The feedback form would be filled out during the homily in order to receive the most instinctive impressions. Forms were handed out in all three parishes before the Eucharist began and those assembled were asked to immediately write down their age at the top of the form. Congregants were then invited to list any words, phrases or metaphors that touched them or were particularly striking to them as the homily was actually being preached. After the homily, they were then instructed to write down what overall message the homily conveyed. A final step was to circle *very, somewhat,* or *not at all* in terms of the homily's relevance to their life. This written instrument would provide the objective measurement of the "test-case" homily.

Focus groups of at least nine people chosen from Pre-Vatican II, Vatican II, and Post-Vatican II cohorts provided a subjective instrument of measurement. Participants gathered immediately following the liturgy. Their instructions were to share the words, phrases and metaphors they had written on their feedback forms and the reasons behind their comments.

C. Homiletic Approach

My exegetical preparation drew primarily from *The New Jerome Biblical Commentary* and *The Collegeville Bible Commentary.* I also used two articles that caught my attention: "Inescapably, Obsessively, Totally Connected: Life in the Wireless Age"[3] and "Gospel Power: Power in the Service of Compassion."[4] Viewed through the lens of the Scriptures, the themes that emerged from these resources provided ample material from which to create an intergenerational homiletic. A broad sweep of the overall thematic running through the homily will be explained.

Reflecting upon the gospel theme of renouncing one's possessions at great cost for the Reign of God, I chose surrendering power as my homiletic focus. Power is, to adapt a popular turn of phrase, the "mother of all possessions." It is the essential means by which we attempt to deal with our finiteness. Yet it is the antithesis of what the Gospel proclaims: our true power rests not in ourselves but in God.

Technology is one of the most familiar ways all generations try to acquire power. A neutral good in itself, its particular appropriation

[3] James Gleick, "Inescapably, Obsessively, Totally Connected: Life in the Wireless Age," *The New York Times Magazine* (April 22, 2001) 62–67.

[4] Dorothy Jonaitis, O.P., "Gospel Power: Power in the Service of Compassion," *Tessera: Dominican Life and Mission Journal* 5, no. 2 (Winter 1995) 9–11.

into our day-to-day lives can be insidious: people begin *using it,* but often it ends up *using them.* The seductive pursuit of power is often a subtle phenomenon because, at its deepest level, it is a "holy search" for connection and fidelity, two spiritual goods natural to the human journey. The Good News underscores this truth offering. It is through the powerlessness of Christian discipleship that we discover connection and fidelity in God's power.

Technological connection is one contemporary, illusory pursuit attempting to substitute for that which only discipleship can give. When pursued indiscriminately, it promotes a wireless prison of perpetual distraction. At the heart of the first reading from the book of Wisdom, this perpetual distraction is the ailment in our "earthen shelter [that] weighs down the mind [with] many concerns" (9:13-18a). Technology is one of the most common intergenerational symbols and symptoms of this unbridled pursuit. Hence, it was used as the guiding metaphor of this intergenerational preaching. A more specific, visual walk through the homily's structure will reveal the mechanics of this approach. The homily opens with the scene of my preteen niece wanting a refrigerator in her room. She was miffed that the request had been denied by disengaged parents who just don't understand. The placement of this story at the beginning is meant not only to immediately draw in the Millennial Generation with a tale about one of their own but also their Baby Boomer parents who wrestle everyday with teenagers' sense of entitlement.

The second paragraph of the homily seeks to hold Baby Boomers' attention while attracting Generation X's attention through the cross generational reference to Star Trek. "Beam me up, Scottie" came of age with the Baby Boomers, but "being a Trekie" is also a Generation X phenomenon through *Nick at Nite* serial reruns. Introducing the technology theme with a common example from their daily culture (e.g., instant messengers) also holds the attention of Millennials. The paragraph ends by interweaving the themes of technology, the distraction that its unbridled pursuit causes, and the gospel message. We are to embrace a discipleship rooted in personal powerlessness for the sake of God's powerfulness within us.

Paragraph 3 delves more deeply into that gospel message by using varied and humorous examples of our society's linguistic preoccupation with power. In a play for the linear Builders and Silent Generations, I first offer Webster's definition of power. Then I juxtapose the varied generational colloquialisms regarding power with Jesus' call to surrender our power and embrace God's. One of the demons that distracts generations from responding to that call is today's *power trip,* being "technologically connected."

From this premise, a *The New York Times Magazine* journalist draws a humorous, but thought-provoking example. Nathan Lane, a comedian familiar to the older generations, is featured with his penchant for technological gadgets from cell phones to palm pilots. This is technology that all generations can relate to. Discipleship is then illustrated as a radically different proposition that nonetheless offers authentic connection rather than the superficial "wireless fidelity" of electronic gadgetry. The pervasive, unconditional witness of faith that Jesus calls for is not built through "remote control theology" but a committed, costly battle with self-renunciation.

Bridge Builders and Silent Generation members can relate to this call for commitment and hard work that require us to put ourselves aside. Discipleship as "not a walk in the park" is an analogical colloquialism that would resonate in their hearing. The phrase that immediately follows, "not a skip through cyberspace," is an attempt to achieve that same resonance with the younger generations. Al Gore's and George Bush's calculating approach to their 2000 campaign battle is an intergenerational example to bring this point home. What we hail as an achievement in computer research, wireless fidelity between all our machines, is juxtaposed against achievement in our spiritual lives: a parallel, wireless, "non-compartmentalized" fidelity to Christ.

This brings us full circle to the heart of the matter for all generations: our natural human quest for the power of connection and fidelity. We seek this possession 24/7/365, a favorite linguistic expression of Generation X that is rapidly becoming popular in other generations' daily lexicons. The Baby Boomer understanding of this dilemma is sought by describing a cultural experience of its generation: office professionals to stay-at-home "soccer moms" experience *surviving* one's life rather than *living* it. The power of connection and fidelity is further explored in the triple "twinning" of the use of technology as an everyday positive that can easily become a negative.

This rhetorical triplet of the positives and negatives of technological power in their specific life experiences is a message directed toward all generations. All five generations can, in some fashion, relate to the high-speed, fast-paced nature of their lives in which lack of time with those they love is a sensitive issue. The older cohorts can identify this phenomenon with the ambiguous blessing of the advent of all day music television (MTV) and the twenty-four-hour news cycle (CNN). Harry Potter, of happy Millennial Generation memory, is pulled in to bring the same point of the dangers of technological obsession to our youngest generational cohort.

The last two paragraphs of the homily summarize the overall homiletic focus and concluding point to all the generations: "If we cannot live without something we have, we no longer have it, it has us!" The fidelity of Jesus' friendship is the authentic connection our hearts seek and the only true source of power in our lives. Therefore, we must relinquish those possessions that possess us and substitute their illusory power for that of God's real power. Only then will we be able to see God's face in those all around us. To make this point poignant for each generation, I chose five specific examples suited to their particular generation worldview:

- The child for Baby Boomers for whom family is so important
- The wife for the older generations who so value long-term commitment
- The grocery store clerk for the Millennials for whom malls have become amusement parks
- The "person without a home" for younger, "social justice-minded" generations
- The employee who is "a person before a worker" illustration for Generation Xers for whom social justice is a passionate concern

The above effort culminates in the trans-generational hub symbol of the Eucharist with an intimate and moving description of the divine gift of Christ as "the kiss of God." At some level, every generation has known the joy of an affirming and loving kiss. This is a powerful image, offered to us each Sunday, in which all of our true power as disciples rests. The Silent Generation and Bridge Builders, for whom the Church teachings on Sunday Mass attendance and the reception of Eucharist are "sacrosanct," would appreciate and resonate with this final reminder. Hopefully, Baby Boomers who are not as faithful in regular church attendance would hear the gentle but clear challenge to greater commitment. They also would appreciate the inclusion of a theology of the Word as another important table from which we feast. Generation Xers and the Millennials would be drawn to this challenge as an invitation to connection and the possibility of belonging to Christ in an intimate and meaningful way. All generations would ideally walk away with the entire point of the preaching in their heads: "Don't get distracted from the kiss God wants to give you each Sunday in Word and Eucharist, for it is your true power and possession in the week that lies ahead!" Table 4 illustrates the hub symbols which target each generation in the homily. The last column reflects my supposition of responses that would most likely be chosen by the five generations within their Catholic generational cohorts. This table also reveals the strategic placement and subtle interweaving of these targeted hub symbols in the project homily (see Appendix 2). This "test case" reflects my book's central contention: one can preach effectively to all generations at the same time in the same setting.

D. Analysis of Data

Let us now examine both the written and oral feedback from the three sites chosen for the "test-case" intergenerational preaching.

1. *Written Feedback*

Data collation and analysis of the written feedback were approached through a five-step process of subdivision. First, each of the three parishes' responses was separately collected. Second, they were divided according to those who responded to the homily as "very" relevant or "somewhat" relevant to their daily lives. Third, the "verys" and the "somewhats" of each parish were divided into five age groupings: Under 14, 14 to 17, 18 to 35, 36 to 59, and 60+ (see Appendix 3: Tables 5, 6, and 7 as well as Graphs 1, 2, and 3). These age groups were categorized according to which of the "verys" and "somewhats" actually heard or failed to hear the intended message of the homily (see Appendix 4: Graphs 4, 5, 6). Because the author-turned-evaluator might reflect bias, a second evaluator was enlisted to confirm or dispute interpretations of respondents' comments. Those disputed were awarded a half point if they survived the second attempt at interpretation by both evaluators. This required at least some clear, although partial, understanding. The standard was whether or not the respondent wrote any or part of the following foci of the homily:

Table 4: Comprehensive Chart with Targeted Hub Symbols

Generations	*Dominant Values*	*Key Characteristics*	*Catholic Generational Cohorts*	*Key Cultural Influences*	*Key Catholic Influences*	***9/8/01 Homiletic "Hub Symbols"***
Builders (1901-1924) *The Institutional Generation*	Dedication/sacrifice	Committed to church; Committed to community	**Pre-Vatican II Church** **(Formed: 1920s, 30s, 40s)**	Prosperity of roaring 20's	Immigrant communities	**"All the way; Not a walk in the park; Can't edit out or jump over"**
	Respect for authority	Linear, uncritical outlook		Depression: Economic hardship	Blue collar/working class	**Definition of Power;** **St. Bernard of Clarvieux**
	Hard Work	Traditional beliefs/practices		WWII: Evils of Nazism	Traditional symbols	**Eucharist: "Kiss of God;" Soul**
	Conformity	Minister out of responsibility Minister out of duty		Help from families and government	Networking organizations	**"fast-traveling disease"**
	Law and Order	Loyalty/Moral obligation to God		Authority conscious	Ghetto mentality	**Campaign battle: George & Al**
	Security/Stability	"Construct a society"		Sought peace/common good	Stressed Church practice	**"Sunday…don't pass it up"**
				Prohibition	Doctrinal uniformity	**Fidelity: "faithful connection"**
				Government Involvement/ The New Deal	Institutional model	**GI Joes**
Silent (1925-1942) *Bridge Builders*	Patience	Committed to Justice Public Good				**Surrender 'possession' for greater good. Face of God: employee**
	Adherence to rules	Conversation/Dialogue				**Campaign: Al and George**
	Duty before pleasure	People-first concern				**"Not a walk in the park;" Soul**
	Delayed reward	Flexibility/Reconciliation				**Fridge, car, tools, washer & dryer**
	Honor	"Keep society together"				**Cell phones**
						Eucharist; St. Bernard of Clarvieux
						"Kiss of God"
Baby Boomers **(1943-1961/64)** *"Visionaries and Seekers"*	Optimism	Seek purpose; Seek community	**Vatican II Church** **(Formed: 1950s, 60s)**	Tranquility of Eisenhower Years	Foot in old /new church	**Wireless Age of Immediacy; Tech-connection: prison of own making; rob time; less connected**
	Team Orientation/pluralistic	Spiritual, not religious		Radical social movements/60s	Baltimore Catechism/Vat. II	**Eucharist: "Kiss of God"**
	Propensity toward confrontation	Family-oriented/community		Respected/Questioned authority	World now "positive"	**"Preteen niece" story**
	Immediate gratification	Democratic, not authoritarian		Civil Rights Movement	Ecumenism/truth expands	**"Remote Control Discipleship"** **Campaign: Al & George; Cell ph.**
	Personal choice/growth	"Justify, purify, sanctify society"		Vietnam War Protests	Guide: Conscience to Church	**Perpetual Distraction**
				Institutions to Individualism	Greater lay involvement	**Power lunch, walk; Power Point**
				Political Assassinations	Classical/historic consciousness	**"Beam me up" CNN; Nathan Lane**
Generation X **(1961/64--1981)** *"A Relational Generation"*	Institutional Disillusionment	Shaped by popular culture	**Post-Vatican II Church** **(Formed: 1970s, 80s)**	Prosperity of roaring 90's	"Virtual Ministry"/Cyberspace	**"Beam me up;" MTV; H. Potter; "skip in cyberspace;" Info flow, perpetual distraction; 24/7/365**
	Technoliteracy	Interactive/nonlinear/critical		Decrease in discrimination	Experiential approach to faith	**Tech-connection; wireless fidelity**
	Self-reliant, but relational	Suspicious of "absolutes"		Increase opportunities for women	Guitar Masses	**Word & Eucharist: "Kiss of God"**
	Informal/pragmatic/tolerant	Relationship vs. accomplishment		Increase environmental concerns	Individualistic faith journey	**"my friendship; your connection"**
	Personal experience/relativistic	"Make *self* right, then society"		Watergate/Whitewater	"Deconstructed context"	**Power at fingertips; Handheld PC**
				3-Mile Island/Chernobyl	Decrease: ritual/obedience	**Totally connected; preteen story**
				Challenger Tragedy	Revival of mysticism	
Millennial (1981-present) *"Young Navigators"*	Optimism	Open to explore, investigate		Fear of AIDS	"Sacramental" in Pop Culture	**Preteen Niece; MTV;** **Power Rangers; H. Potter; Legos; GI Joes**
	Confidence/sociability	Being connected		Increased divorce	More Christian than Catholic	**Tech; "I am that connection"**
	Morality/"street-smarts"	Multi-media savvy/imaginal		Vietnam to Iran	Favor Social Justice	**Skip-cyberspace; "at ten for 'IM"**
	Civic-Duty/achievement			No Middle Class	Multiple *Catholic* expressions	**24/7/365**
	Diversity	Service/ "do my part socially"		High unemployment/ hugh income gap	Campus Newman Centers	**The power of my friendship; Kiss of God-Eucharist**
				Distrust authorities/ religion as social institution	Desire democratic model	**Information flow/perpetual distraction**
						Cf: John Roberto & Robert Allen

1. Don't get distracted in the pursuit of your own power (i.e., technology) and pass up your true power and possession in Christ.
2. In His faithful friendship is where your most authentic connection lies.

The final subdivision specified most commonly mentioned hub symbols for each of these groups (see Appendix 5: Tables 8, 9, 10). Once individually sorted, the data from the three parishes was combined to form a picture of the whole in each of the subdivisions (see Appendices 6, 7, 8 in the following order: Table 11, Graph 7, Table 12, and Graph 8).

The written feedback clearly and substantially confirms the foundation of this book's thesis: *every generation can be preached to effectively at the same time in the same setting by using a variety of generation-specific "cues," references or targeted hub symbols.* Out of 598 respondents, 579 indicated that the homily was either "very" or "somewhat" relevant. Of those, 395 circled "very" under the question measuring relevancy. Every group except the under-14 category (separated by one point), ranked the homily as "very" relevant more often than "somewhat" relevant. For those age ranges that provided the bulk of the written feedback, the 18 to 35 group with 168 returned surveys and the 35 to 59 group with 271, the homily was considered "very relevant" by at least a two to one majority.

The two age categories mentioned above also scored highest in understanding the intended message of the homily, whether they found it "very" or only "somewhat" relevant.[5] Those in the 60+ and the 14 to 17 category also understood the homily's message, but with less than a two to one ratio. Every age range overwhelmingly heard the homiletic message intended by the preacher. Predictably, only those who found the preaching "not at all" relevant to their lives tended not to understand the homily's message.

The reactions to the targeted hub symbols within the homily highlight both the strengths and challenges of intergenerational preaching. Approximately one out of four found the homily "somewhat"

[5] The graph reads as follows: the first color in each bar of the three relevancy measurement categories (i.e., blue for the "very" relevant scorers) represents those who heard the intended message. The second color in the bar (i.e., the maroon in the "very") represents those in the same group who did not hear the intended message.

relevant and the majority of those who found it "not at all" relevant took issue with the number of images, metaphors and familiar turns of phrases. Interestingly enough, this was the very technique that those who found the preaching "very" relevant commended! However, even here there were several who, while applauding the specific effort to reach all generations, wondered if there were too many examples. Yet, others in the "very" category felt the many images and metaphors kept their interest and made the homily easy to follow.

It appears that what is too much for one person and distracts from the message is the very element that keeps the attention of another. The tension is reflected in the seemingly contradictory comments of two respondents, one advising: "explain more," while the other warns: "don't spoon feed." Clearly, a great challenge for intergenerational preaching is intuiting "how much is too much."

In terms of the final subdivision of the data highlighting common hub symbols, combined results were mostly predictable with only a few unpredictable connections. The phrase "Let go of your power and embrace mine" was the most frequently cited "hub symbol" in age ranges 18 to 35 and 36 to 59, and the second most popular choice in age grouping 14 to 17. It spoke powerfully across three generations. The "Kiss of God" image and quote of St. Bernard of Clairveaux also spoke across three generations. It was most popular, as predicted and targeted, with the 60+ group but also close to number one in popularity with the 14 to 17 and 36 to 59 age cohorts.

While the specific phrases varied from "Perpetual distraction" to "Don't get distracted," the key theme of distraction had been successfully triggered. Even the "very and somewhat relevant" homily responders under age fourteen picked phrases that clearly reflected this central focus of the homily. Most popular of all the hub symbol phrases were "Let go of possessions that possess you" and "Don't get distracted." A close third that also appeared cross-generationally was "basement of the soul." Most popular words included: power, distraction, discipleship, and "Let go." A frequently recorded phrase that was not part of my targeted hub symbols but reflected a reoccurring theme of the homily was, "Let go and let God." This analysis represents the broad sweep of the homily's impact. Now let's look at the specific evidence linking the preacher's targeted hub symbols to their intended hearers.

Table 13 (see Appendix 9) measures the strength of correlation between strategically placed hub symbols and their reception by hearers within their respective Catholic generational cohorts and age groupings. These individual generations are roughly equivalent to the Catholic generational cohorts, with two age categories comprising both Pre-Vatican II and Post-Vatican cohorts.[6] The shaded first column in the table lists the preacher's specifically targeted hub symbols developed for each generational cohort prior to the intergenerational preaching. The next three consecutive columns provide analysis of hub symbol impact by listing the percentage of response frequency per parish in the test case study. The last two small columns offer a snapshot view of overall popularity of a particular hub symbol (word, image or phrase) within a particular cohort and overall popularity with all respondents across cohorts. Several observations are readily discernable within each Catholic generational cohort.

Formed Pre-Vatican II (60+):

- One of every five people understood the homiletic message through the hub symbol: "Can't edit out or jump over those parts we don't like."
- Five more targeted hub symbols were recognized by at least one out of every three people. These included: the word/image "connection," the phrase, "Sunday . . . Don't get distracted and pass . . .," "Kiss of God," the word/image, "Power," and the phrase, "basement of the soul."
- The hub symbol phrase, "basement of the soul," was cited by one of every two people.
- The word/image, "power in" its various analogies and references, was reported by seventeen of twenty people.

Formed during Vatican II (36 to 59):

- One of every five responded to the hub symbol phrase, "Wireless Age of Immediacy/wireless fidelity," the word/image, "connection," and the targeted hub symbol: "remote-control discipleship."

[6] This delineation breaks out in the following manner: age 60+ represents Builders and Silent generations formed Pre-Vatican II, 36- to 59-year-old Baby Boomers formed during Vatican II, and Post-Vatican II Generation X and Millennial ages 35 and under.

- Three more hub symbols: "Kiss of God" and the word/images: "distraction" and "power" were noted by two of every five people.
- Similar in popularity to the 60+ group, this latter word/image, "power," was cited by twenty-two of every twenty-five people.

Formed Post-Vatican II (35 and under):

- One of every 4.5 people responded to the "Kiss of God" hub symbol and the targeted word/image, "connection."
- Three more strategically placed hub symbols were reported by at least one out of every three people in this cohort: the word/image, "distraction," "Wireless Age of Immediacy/wireless fidelity, and the word/image," "power."
- Two of every five respondents recorded the word/image "distraction."
- Again, the word/image, "power," was the strongest hub symbol reported by all cohorts. For the 35 and under group, it was noted by one of every two people.

What is readily apparent from the strength of these targeted hub symbols within their respective cohorts is that the preacher's expectations were confirmed and the strategic placement of words, images and phases according to generation, was highly successful. The overall statistical analysis also yielded interesting and confirming results.

All Catholic Generational Cohorts:

- Three of every four people reported the word/image, "power," within the total respondents of all cohorts.
- Two of every five people responded to the word/image, "distractions," in its various uses.
- Another above-average showing across Catholic generational cohorts was the word/image, "connection," with a response of 27 percent.
- The popularity of the hub symbol "Kiss of God" is also evident in the strong response it was given by 36 percent of respondents across all cohorts.

Probably most striking is that four hub symbols out of the overall categories were reported by at least one out of every four respondents, with some much higher.

The above percentages clearly demonstrate the effectiveness of the test-case intergenerational preaching through specific, targeted hub symbols that spoke to the generation for which they were intended. This supports the heart of this book's thesis: generation-specific words, images and phrases make true intergenerational preaching possible and credible when included as an integral part of homiletic preparation.

2. *Oral Feedback*

Following the liturgies at all three parishes, a focus group of at least nine people was convened. Each group consisted of three representatives of Pre-Vatican II, Vatican II, and Post-Vatican II. The purpose of these gatherings was to gain insight into the reasoning behind the written data. In other words, why would someone from a particular Catholic generational cohort respond to a particular targeted hub symbol? No new questions were asked of these random representatives. Instead, they were asked to specifically state why a phrase they wrote struck them. An impartial facilitator led and audiotaped the group discussion. Two parishes, St. Jerome and St. Peter, provided adequate and measurable feedback. Unfortunately, Washington University's audiotape was not discernable.

Out of thirteen respondents from St. Peter parish (see Appendix 10), eight people from all three cohorts clearly understood the message and relevancy of the homily. An eighty-year-old woman reported that she "isn't much into technology and had trouble hearing most of it." The hub symbols that were most striking to the rest of the group in their respective age groupings from fourteen to seventy were strongly consistent with the pattern of the written feedback. Hub symbols phrases "Perpetual distraction" and "Kiss of God" as well as the word/images "power" and "connection" were repeatedly cited by those generational cohorts to which they were targeted.

Four Post-Vatican teenagers, ages fourteen to sixteen, participated in the group. Their contribution centered on the words, images or phrases that touched them, rather than direct statements about the homily's relevance. Their comments also followed the pattern of the written feedback for the Post-Vatican cohort. This infers that they also understood the thrust of the preaching. Three mentioned two targeted hub symbols, respondents, and three also cited technology examples, two specifically for their age group.[7]

Out of nine respondents at St. Jerome, the overwhelming majority clearly understood the homily's message and relevancy. Their comments also reflected strong consistency with the written feedback. The hub symbol phrases that most captured their attention were, "Let go of possessions that possess you," "basement of the soul" and "Kiss of God" as well as the consistently popular word/image, "power." While no young people spoke directly, those in the Vatican II cohort affirmed that their teenagers were responding in writing as the homily was delivered and that "Harry Potter" was one targeted symbol they thought was particularly effective for their children.

Having established a high consistency with the study's written results, the focus groups also explored more deeply why people of both parishes felt compelled to write particular hub symbols. The fact that the targeted words, images and phrases were drawn from their everyday experience was the consistent reason given for their strong impact. Numerous comments are revealing:

- "Everyday visuals were used that we could really relate to . . . technology [as an example] would appeal to a lot of ages."
- "We need to hear homilies . . . and I think that Father did this . . . that relate to everyday life, for example, our relationships with one another."
- "Perpetual distraction . . . all the power analogies . . . ties/suits distract us from what the true power is . . . liked that he [homilist] brought all that in."
- The "refrigerator story . . . related to everyday life."
- "PDAs and cell phones . . . why do we need that? You can get by without it. We have what we need—God as our connection."
- "When I heard remote-control discipleship, I thought if that isn't the truth . . . and that 'Kiss of God' image . . . thought that was interesting, but after Communion, it really hit me!"

[7] The targeted hub symbols were: (1) Harry Potter and (2) "I'll meet you on line at ten for an IM (instant message)."

Using everyday images also appealed to the Millennial Generation. Keith, a fourteen-year-old Post-Vatican II Catholic, had this to share from his everyday experience: "IMs and computers . . . that's how I talk to my friends." Amy, a sixteen- year-old teen, was drawn in by the cell phone example: "Everyone in high school has one."[8]

A member of the Vatican II cohort noted how the preaching resonated with her common, everyday conversations: "My best friend does Power Point Presentations and we always talk about Star Trek." Another member of the same cohort reflected: "We keep giving our children more and more and then they expect more; you really are not free . . . 'wireless fidelity,' oh, that's so true!"

Finally, a Pre-Vatican II, St. Jerome participant affirmed a St. Peter's focus group member's observation. They both agreed that use of the hub symbol phrase "basement of the soul" was "a visual that makes you dig deeper. Maybe it means more to our generation [60+] because basements are different . . . they are all more fixed up today than they were in my day."

While overall comments from both groups were exceedingly positive, there were hints in the St. Jerome group that a good thing was carried too far. These people indicated that the homily was "a barrage" of metaphors and images that, at times, felt overwhelming. Conversely, a participant at St. Peter praised this very attribute of the homily. He lauded the effort to "pepper the message with vivid pieces and catch phrases . . . because it is important to catch [and hold] our attention. One big message runs the risk of losing us if we don't catch all the parts." The amount of metaphor usage is a continuing debate but appears to be in the eyes of the beholder.

In retrospect, I agree that fewer metaphors or images could have been just as effective. But often that's what happens when you get so excited about experimenting with a new idea or innovative approach! One can be tempted to overdo a good thing. So be mindful of taking a good technique too far. The paramount concern for intergenerational preaching is to be sure to proclaim God's Word in metaphorical images that include and engage all generations.

Overall, the oral feedback clearly suggested that people responded to their individual experience and collective generational milieu. The gospel message was revealed through words, images, and phrases, and

[8] For additional comments with specific ages of respondents, refer to Appendix 9.

the intentional generational translation of these for their daily lives. Thus, the truth of the Scriptures came alive for them.

Both parishes mentioned above appreciated the preacher's intent to speak to all generations. Almost everyone present acknowledged that all generations were included with special mention by parents on how this approach benefited their children as well as themselves.

So What? 7

As the pastor in the story at the beginning of the last chapter pointed out, most preaching is, pragmatically speaking, intergenerational because the congregation is intergenerational. However, it is critical that the preacher's homiletic preparation take this practical reality into consideration. Strategically and intentionally, this means using different symbols to reach different generations. As I said earlier, one size *does not* fit all. A cookie-cutter approach to preaching that merely "throws mud at the wall hoping some will stick," doesn't work. This is neither responsible nor respectful to the generations present in the congregation. Intended or not, when the Word is preached without serious effort to draw from various generational lexicons, the message invariably is sent that

- "I don't see you."
- "You are not important."
- "You are not on my radar screen."
- "You are invisible to me."

The artful craft of intergenerational preaching is most poignantly highlighted when one message is effectively and credibly mediated to a variety of persons through generational symbols. This requires solid exegesis, thorough congregational analysis and an educated, ongoing awareness of generation-specific symbols. Most preachers learn the first tools of exegesis in seminary, but little or no time is spent on developing other necessary skills. I offer the following suggestions to preachers who are either permanently assigned to a congregation or routinely provide support to a particular assembly:

A. Develop a Four-step Intergenerational Chart for Homiletic Preparation:

1. Utilizing parish statistics, exegete your congregation according to age groupings and cultural experience along generational lines. This generational segmentation of the assembly should show what percentage of the congregation falls into each age group.[1]
2. Chart your findings for handy use when engaged in homiletic preparation.
3. Add to the chart three Catholic generational cohorts: Pre-Vatican I, Vatican II, and Post-Vatican II. List the characteristics of these varied cohorts within these divisions.
4. Make a final column on the same chart and leave it blank. This chart with the general cultural characteristics of each generation, their formative traits within each Catholic cohort and a place to list effective hub symbols according to that weekend's specific preaching will be an invaluable resource during homiletic preparation.[2]

B. Build a Generational Lexicon:

- Make a glossary of terms and common "turns of phrase" routinely used by different age cohorts.

C. Organize a Generational Preacher's Notebook:

1. Subdivisions of the notebook are organized according to generational cohorts. Collect artifacts, concepts and behaviors as part of each generation's cultural deposit.[3] Draw from newspapers, magazines, novels, movies and Internet resources.
2. Organize Catholic cohorts in the preacher's notebook. How might Catholic news affect each cohort? Read Catholic sources for ideas.

[1] This may vary from Mass to Mass.
[2] Refer to chart completed for this thesis project in Chapter 5.
[3] Refer to Chapter 2.

D. Develop Generational Profiles:

- Maintain and update ongoing composites of each of the five major generations comprising your assembly.

At the end of a homiletics practicum one day, my professor startled her student preachers with, "So what?" She was echoing Protestant homiletics guru Fred Craddock's famous directive that preachers should ask this question as a final check on a prepared preaching's relevancy. "So what?" gets at the heart of both relevancy and credibility.

This book has explored both the theory and practical application of intergenerational preaching. I have argued for the practical intersection of language and culture within the reality of diverse generational identities. I have proposed a homiletic approach that embraces a qualified segmentation based on the subculture of generation and the formative experience of Catholic generational cohorts, with special emphasis on the Catholic sacramental imagination. Results from my "test case" preaching strongly suggest that as a homiletic device, generational targeting is a very promising, although not precise, instrument. At this point, we might ask "So what?"

People respond to everyday life phenomena out of their generational identities, formed through similar historical experiences that have shaped their lifelong character and values. Just as generational viewpoints play a highly influential role in the spending habits of consumers, they significantly impact how people engage with a homily.

If the goal is to preach the Word of God in an optimal way, an intergenerational preaching homiletic offers an effective approach to negotiate generational boundaries within a local parish and sustain generational commitment within the larger church. Preachers utilizing the above suggestions can confidently, competently, and credibly address the diverse outlooks of those generations filling church pews Sunday after Sunday. In times of crisis, church attendance is strong.[4] If such attendance is to become an ongoing reality, this homiletic is one way to nurture varied generations' faith formation and institutional involvement.

In the final analysis, intergenerational preaching for the authentic proclaimer and preacher of God's Word is not an arbitrary option. If

[4] September 11, 2001, terrorist attacks on the World Trade Center Towers in New York City and the Pentagon in Washington, D.C.

preachers charged with sharing the Christian Vision hope to be effective and competent in reaching persons in different generations, their preaching cannot be developed in a generational vacuum. An intergenerational preaching homiletic provides the lens through which to view the varied cultural and specifically Catholic life journeys of each generation as well as the means to meet the challenge of becoming *generationally indigenous*.[5] Like any art, it requires a committed discipline and an intentional focus.

If we are to be true to the passage in the Eucharistic Preface that says, "in every age, God raises up holy men [and women]," we must preach responsibly to the multiple generations that comprise the Church within every age. A theological approach to Catholic preaching that understands the homily as a unifying act centered in a sacred Christian tradition of two millennia must include in its equation the varied generations who are its faithful disciples.

In the final analysis, true Catholic intergenerational preachers are those who do the homework necessary to readily imagine and authentically address the worldviews of fourteen-year-old Millennials, the pains and joys of thirty-three-year-old Gen-Xers, the disappointments and hopes of forty-eight-year-old Baby Boomers, the regrets and triumphs of sixty-eight-year-old members of the Silent Generation and the eighty-three-year-old Builder's heart-seeking contentment in old age. Then, while looking out from the pulpit, preachers will know that they have effectively and responsibly preached the Word of God to all generations in the congregation. In the end, that is the most important answer to the question, "So what?"

[5] Refer to Chapter 2.

Appendix 1

Parish Feedback Form

Intergenerational Preaching Study	Gender (circle)	Age (check one)
Rev. Andrew Carl Wisdom, O.P.	M F	Under 14 ___
Sunday, September 9, 2001		14 to 17 ___
Feedback Sheet		18 to 35 ___
		36 to 59 ___
		60+ ___

As part of this project, I am gathering data on how homilists can be more effective in preaching to a variety of generations in the same setting. Your comments will provide valuable feedback toward that effort. As you listen to the homily, please write down any ***words, phrases,*** or ***metaphors*** that *strike* or *touch* you. Feel free to write down as many or as few as you wish. Thank you very much for your help!

(Answer after homily is completed)
Overall, what message did this homily convey to you?

How relevant was that message to your life? (Circle)

Very Somewhat Not at All

Appendix 2
Intergenerational Preaching: A "Test Case"

Twenty-Third Sunday in Ordinary Time
September 2001
Readings: Wisdom 9:13-18a, Ps 90
Philemon 9–10, 12–17
Luke 14:25-33

My preteen niece Katie called one day to complain about her mother: "Your sister is being mean to me!" "Well, that's funny," I said, "she seemed like such a nice person when we were growing up. What's the scoop?" "She won't let me have a refrigerator!" "Well, honey, don't you already have one?" A long, "get with it, Uncle" sigh, and then: "In my room, Uncle Andy! It's rude to leave my guests and go all the way downstairs."

Well, "beam me up, Scottie!" cuz I don't know where I have landed! Who can know God's mind, the book of Wisdom muses?! I'm still trying to figure out my niece's! Welcome to a strange, new galaxy: The Wireless Age of Immediacy, whose inhabitants don't just want but presume power at their fingertips; whose "instant messengers" "will meet you on line at ten for an IM"; who expect connection by walking across the room, not by stepping out of their comfort zone to go "all the way" downstairs. Yet, an "all-the-way" disciple is precisely what Jesus calls for in today's gospel. "To get" what Jesus means and what, as our first reading puts it, "burdens us," you and I need to go downstairs all the way to the basement of our souls to see what, in this "earthen shelter," weighs down our mind.

The essential possession Jesus is asking us to surrender is also our greatest temptation in today's Wireless Age: our insatiable, distracted desire for personal power—power over ourselves, over each other, over the events and circumstances of our lives. Now Mr. Webster defines power as, "possession of control or influence over others." Listen to our everyday language: Professionals talk of power lunches, power ties & suits, and the all-important Power Point presentation. Kids talk of Power Rangers, the State, of Powerball; fitness gurus of a Powerbar before your Power Yoga; and moms of their ever-critical Power Walks, after, of course, what comes first, their power-shopping! Into all of this Jesus says: "LET GO of the focus on your power! Embrace mine!" Never is that challenge more jarring than in today's power trip with being "technologically connected."

A recent newsmagazine headline read: Inescapably, Obsessively, Totally Connected! Comedian Nathan Lane was pictured relaxing under a palm tree on a deserted island. But, peeping up in the sand was a handheld PC, cell phone, portable fax machine, and palm pilot! Gadgets, our journalist said, that "will offer the kind of power over [our lives] that the remote control gives us over TV: the power to edit and jump."

My friends, we cannot remote control discipleship! We can't edit out or jump over those parts we don't like, even if, as Jesus says, they offend our nearest and dearest! To be "a Christ-follower" is a radical all-the-way proposition. Discipleship is not "a walk in the park." It's not a skip through cyberspace. A Christian's life is not a tower built with Legos or a battle waged with GI Joes! Surely Al and George did not build their campaign battle without calculating the odds. Nor should we fail to consider what it takes to build a pervasive witness of faith.

Current computer research, in fact, is all geared toward "pervasive computing." The goal: to insure that all your various electronic gadgets will collectively communicate your needs to each other without bothering you. (My niece Katie would love this!) From a small base headquartered in your home, your various machines will be able to talk to one another through an invisible radiation field. "Your fridge, your car, your tools, your clothes [will be] doing all those microelemental tasks you used to do. Gurus call it: 'wireless fidelity.'" What if that kind of fidelity to Christ pervaded all of our life's roles and responsibilities?

Connection and fidelity. As human beings, we crave the power to possess both. And to quench that thirst, we are all running 24/7/365. But our blind pursuits "edit out" that which truly feeds us. We no longer experience ourselves as living our lives but surviving them. Why? "The dream of perfect information flow can slip easily into a nightmare of perfect perpetual distraction."

Perpetual distraction is the crisis of our MTV/CNN age. It is the invisible poison that destroys our focus on God as our true connection. Like a fast-traveling disease, it eats away at the insides of our individual, family and societal souls. Technology as: "the power of progress?" Hm. . . . Does our use of it give us time or rob us of time; make us more available or less connected to each other; free us up or hold us up in a wireless prison of our own making? Like our British boy wizard Harry Potter, we can be hostages in our own homes, unaware of a higher power within.

Brothers and Sisters, if we cannot live without something we have, we no longer have it, it has us! Too many things "have us" today, distracting us from the only authentic connection that gives us life. Jesus says: "Enough already! I am that faithful connection you are looking for. Follow me, all the way and discover what your restless heart has always sought: the power of my friendship." Friends, Jesus calls us today to let go of possessions that possess us, that distract us from God's face: in the child who longs for a parent's hug, the wife who yearns for the words, "I love you just because," the grocery store clerk who needs your smile this day, the person without a home who too often becomes just another part of the landscape, the employee who is a person before a worker. These people among us are nothing less than the towering presence of Christ here and now, in this place, amid these circumstances of our lives.

Ten centuries ago, St. Bernard of Clarevieux "got that" and wrote: "Christ was given to us as the kiss of God." You and I receive that kiss every time we gather at these tables of Word and Eucharist. Savor the "kiss of God" in the Eucharist today, knowing that Christ is your greatest power and possession in everyplace that connects your Monday to Saturday. As for Sunday, that same "kiss of God" will be here waiting for you. Don't get distracted and pass it up!

Appendix 3

Table 5: St. Jerome Total Respondents				
	VERY	SOMEWHAT	NOT AT ALL	Total
Under 14	10	10	1	**21**
14–17	9	6	0	**15**
18–35	10	2	0	**12**
36–59	57	29	0	**96**
60+	19	16	1	**36**

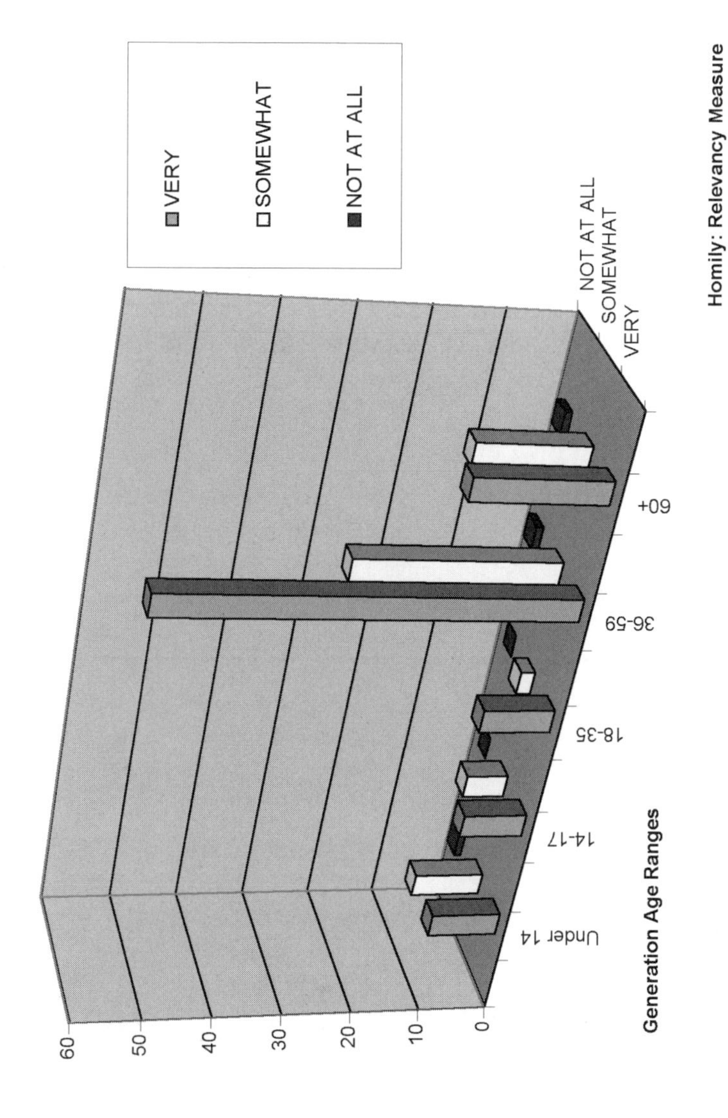
Graph 1: ST. JEROME TOTAL RESPONDENTS
VERY
SOMEWHAT
NOT AT ALL
60
50
40
30
20
10
0
Under 14
14-17
18-35
36-59
60+
VERY
SOMEWHAT
NOT AT ALL
Generation Age Ranges
Homily: Relevancy Measure
Total Number in Category

Table 6:
St. Peter Total Respondents

	VERY	SOMEWHAT	NOT AT ALL	Total
Under 14	3	3	1	**7**
14–17	3	2	0	**5**
18–35	14	8	0	**22**
36–59	77	18	1	**96**
60+	23	22	4	**49**

Graph 2: ST. PETER TOTAL RESPONDENTS

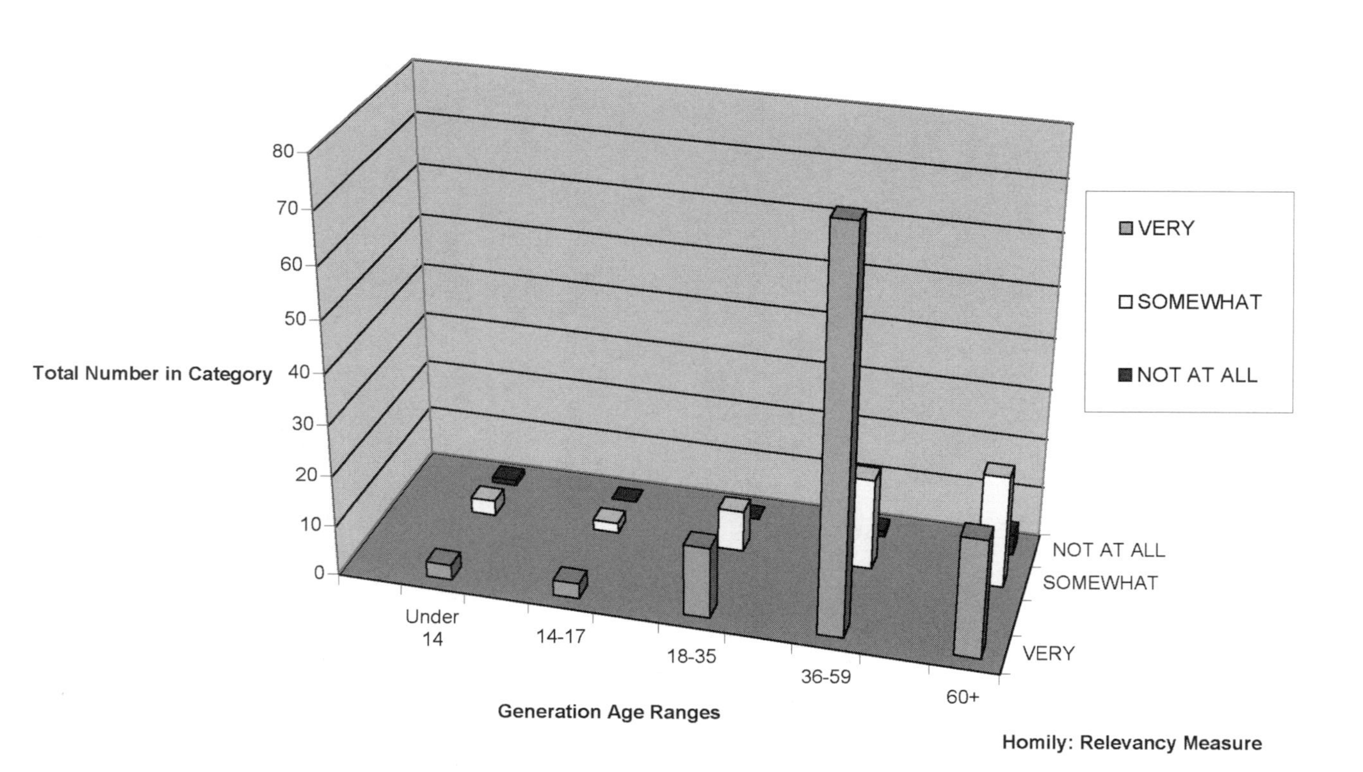

Table 7:
Washington University Total Respondents

	VERY	SOMEWHAT	NOT AT ALL	Total
Under 14	1	2	0	3
14–17	1	2	0	3
18–35	98	43	5	146
36–59	68	20	1	99
60+	12	3	0	15

Graph 3: WASHINGTON UNIVERSITY TOTAL RESPONDENTS

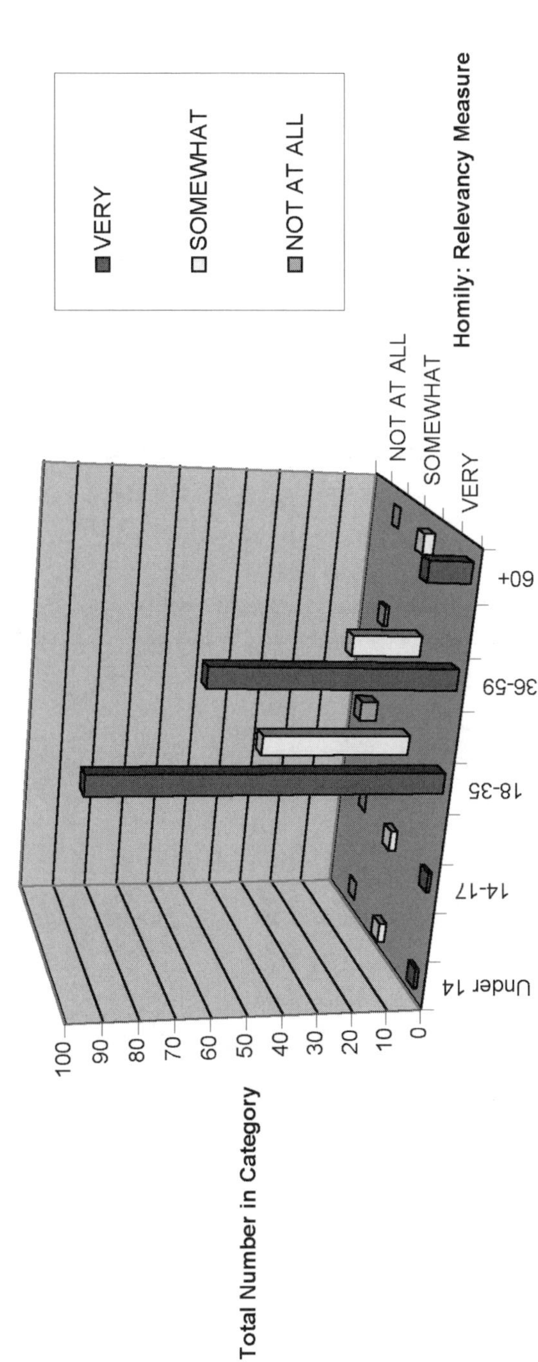

Appendix 4

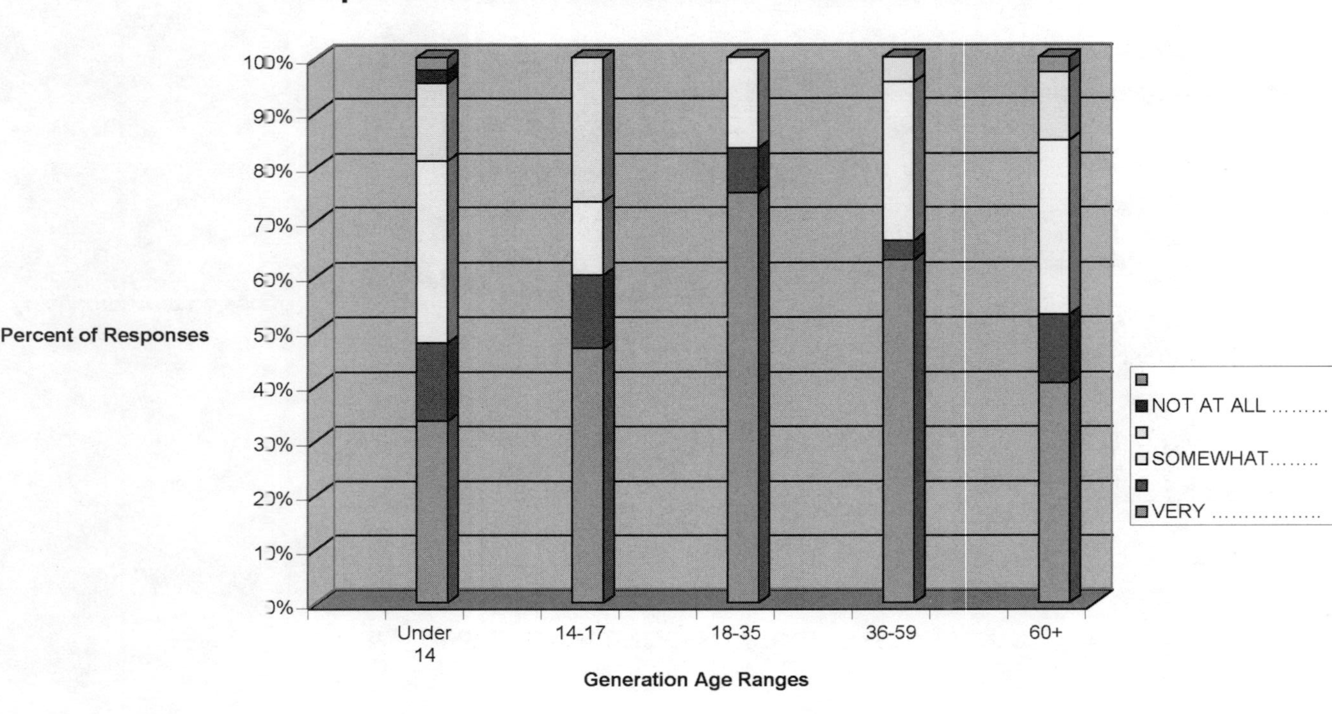
Graph 4: ST. JEROME UNDERSTANDING OF HOMILY MESSAGE
100%
90%
80%
70%
60%
50%
40%
30%
20%
10%
0%
Percent of Responses
Under 14
14-17
18-35
36-59
60+
Generation Age Ranges
NOT AT ALL
SOMEWHAT
VERY

Graph 5: ST. PETER UNDERSTANDING OF HOMILY MESSAGE

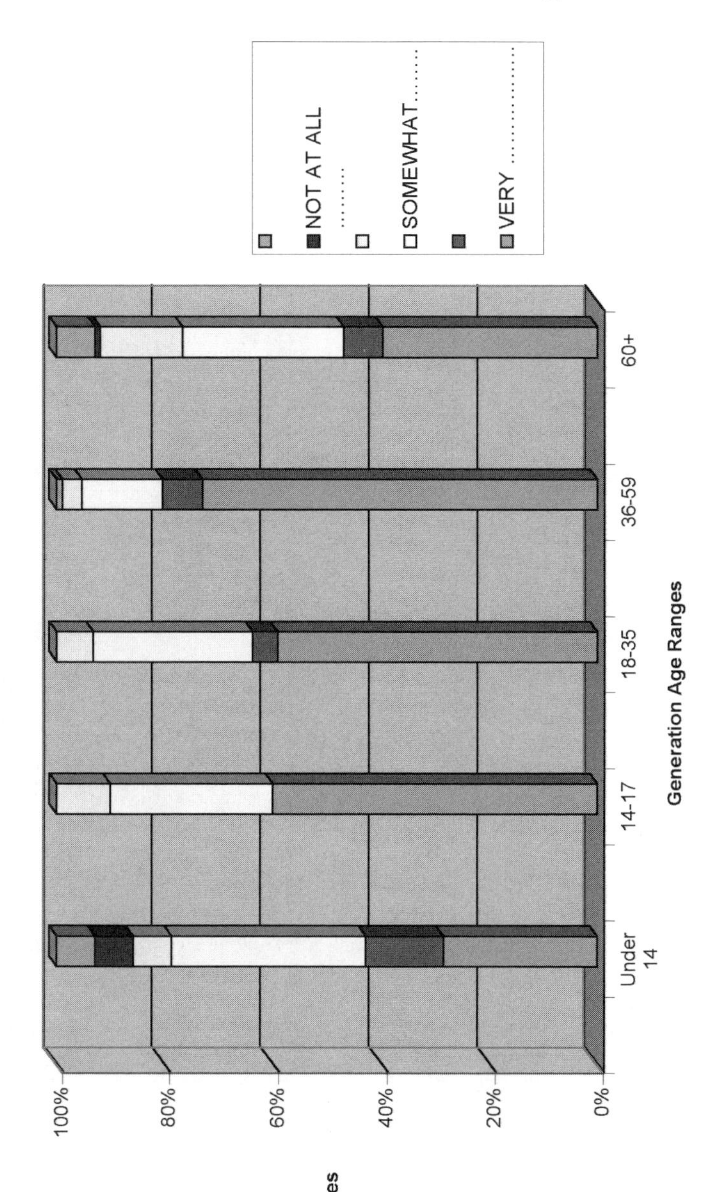

Graph 6: WASHINGTON UNIVERSITY UNDERSTANDING OF HOMILY MESSAGE

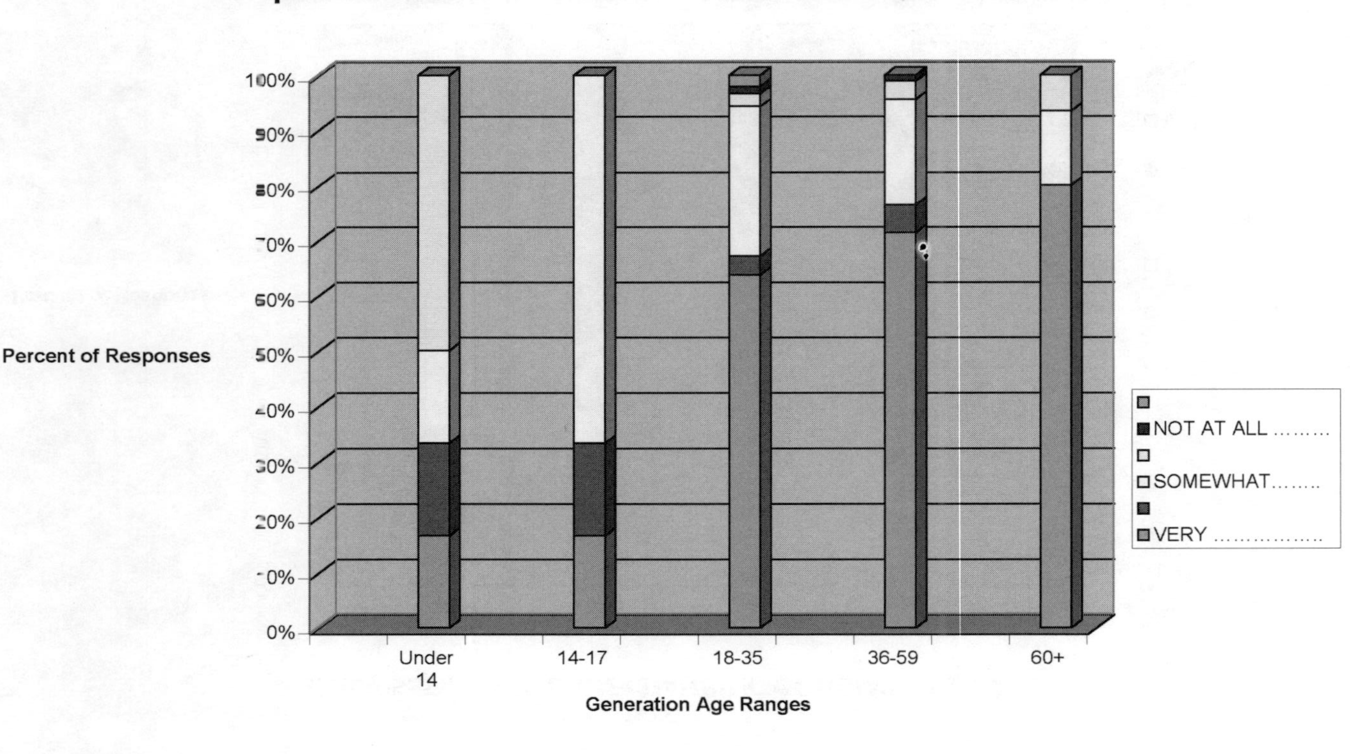

Appendix 5

Table 8: St. Jerome Homiletic Hub Symbols

Age Ranges	"Very" Relevant Responses	"Somewhat" Relevant Responses
Under 14	"Kiss of God" (A); "basement of the soul" (B); "desire for personal power" (C); "Let go of possessions that possess us" (D); "Don't get distracted" (E); "Perpetual Distraction" (F)	(G); (C); (E); Legos; "all the way" (I); Harry Potter
14–17	(E); (B); "pervasive witness of faith" (J); "can't edit or jump over"; (A); "Let go of your power, embrace mine" (G); "free us up or hold us up"	(E); (I)
18–35	(B); "I am that faithful connection" (H); (G)	"Like H. Potter . . . hostages in our own home" (G); (H); (I)
36–59 **36–59**	(B); (C); (A); (G); (F); "not living our lives, but surviving them"; "Beam me up, Scottie"	(E); (D); (C); (B); "comfort zone"; (F); Power examples: lunch, walk, point
60+	(C); (A); (H); (D); "Connection and fidelity"	(C); (H); (E); "possessions asked to surrender"; (J); (A)

Table 9: St. Peter Homiletic Hub Symbols

Age Ranges	"Very" Relevant Responses	"Somewhat" Relevant Responses
Under 14	"Like H.P., prisoners in own home"; "technological connection"; "Let go of possessions that possess us" (A)	"Don't get distracted"; (C); "remote control discipleship" (H); "Let go"
14–17	Discipleship; "Let go of your power, embrace mine" (B)	None listed
18–35	"Kiss of God" (C); (B); "Wireless Age of Immediacy" (I); "If you can't live without something you have, you no longer have it, it has you" (D); "desire for personal power" (K); "Let go of possessions that possess us" (E)	"Wireless fidelity"; (G); "Totally Connected"; (H)
36–59	(C); Power examples: "lunch, walk, point" (J); (B); "only authentic connection" (F); (D); "basement of the soul" (G)	(E); (J); "Beam me up, Scottie"; (I); (C); (G)
60+	(C); (D); "not living our lives, but surviving"; "Perpetual Distraction" (L); (F); (G)	(C); (K); (B); (L); (G)

Table 10: Washington University Homiletic Hub Symbols

Age Ranges	"Very" Relevant Responses	"Somewhat" Relevant Responses
Under 14	None listed	None listed
14–17	"Kiss of God" (A)	"Let go of your power, embrace mine" (B); "desire for personal power" (C)
18–35	(B); (C) "not living our lives, but surviving" (H); "all the way" (M); "Let go of possessions that possess us" (D); "Don't get distracted" (E); (A); "Perpetual Distraction" (F); "Wireless Age of Immediacy" (K); "remote control discipleship" (G); "can't edit or jump over" (J); "If you can't live without something you have, you no longer have it, it has you" (I); "I am that connection"; "face of God"; "rob time; less connected" "pervasive witness of faith" (L)	(C); (B); (D); (A); (F); (E); "basement of the soul" (N); (G); (H); (I)
36–59	(C); (B); (D); (J); (F); (K); "Connection and fidelity"	(D); (A); (C); Power examples: lunch, walk, point; (I); (F); (L); (M)
60+	(B); (A); (C); (N); (J); (K); (F)	(D)

Appendix 6

Table 11: Combined Site Respondents				
	VERY	SOMEWHAT	NOT AT ALL	Total
Under 14	14	15	2	**31**
14–17	13	10	2	**25**
18–35	112	51	5	**168**
36–59	202	67	2	**271**
60+	54	41	5	**100**
Total	395	184	16	**595**

Graph 7: COMBINED SITE RESPONDENTS

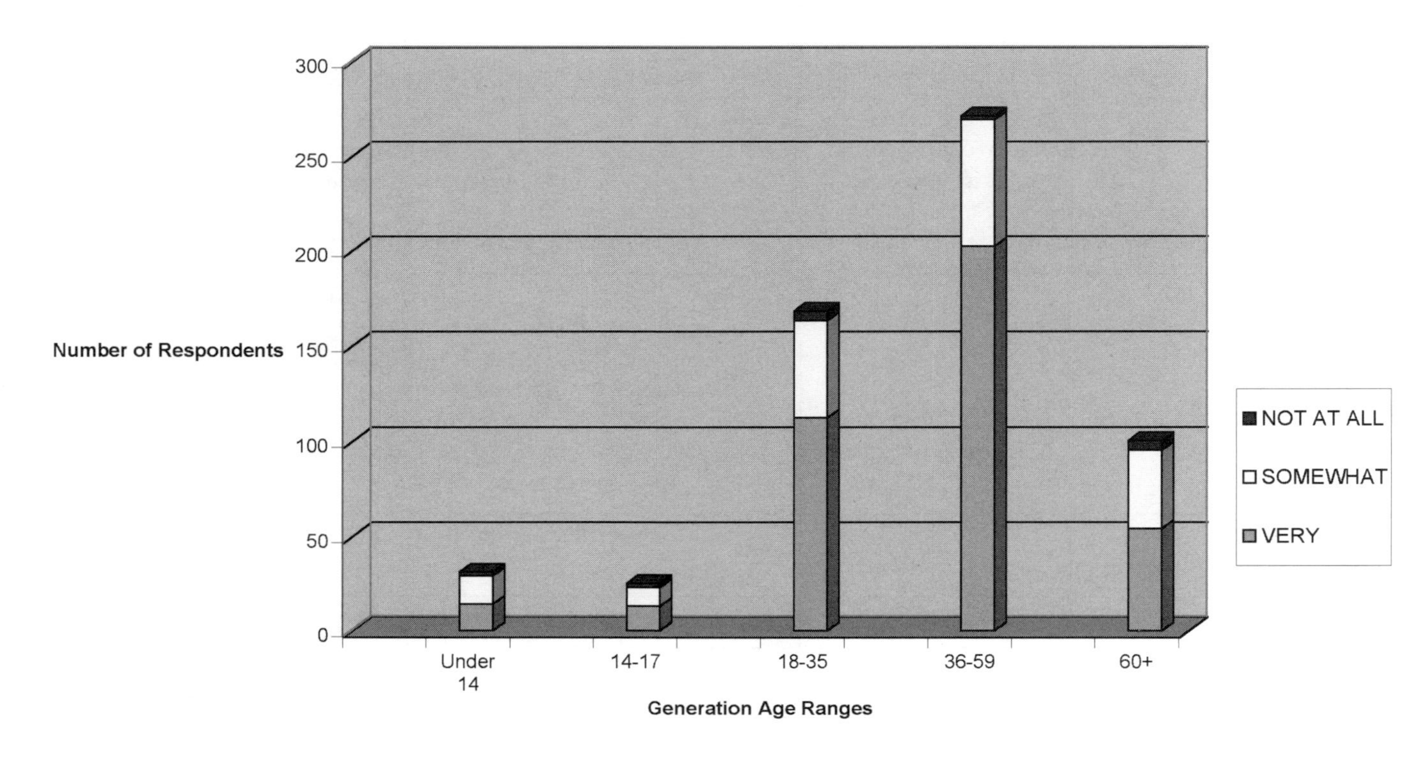

Appendix 7

Table 12: Combined Homiletic Hub Symbols

Age Ranges	"Very" Relevant Responses	"Somewhat" Relevant Responses
Under 14	"Let go of possessions that possess you"	"Don't get distracted"
14–17	"Kiss of God"; "Let go of . . . your power, embrace mine"	No common hub symbols discernable
18–35	* "Let go of . . . your power, embrace mine"; "Let go of possessions that possess us"; "Wireless Age of Immediacy"; "If you can't live without something you have, you no longer have it, it has you"; "I am that faithful connection"; "desire for personal power"	"Let go of . . . your power, embrace mine"; "basement of the soul"; "remote control discipleship"
36–59	* "Let go of . . . your power, embrace mine"; "Kiss of God"; Power examples: lunch, walk, point; "Perpetual Distraction"; "basement of the soul"	* Power examples: lunch, walk, point; * "Let go of possessions that possess us"; "Perpetual Distraction"; "desire for personal power"; "Don't get distracted"
60+	* "Kiss of God"; "I am that faithful connection"; "basement of the soul"; "Perpetual Distraction"	"Don't get distracted"; "desire for personal power"

* = Common hub symbol of all three parishes

Appendix 8

Graph 8: COMBINED UNDERSTANDING OF HOMILY MESSAGE

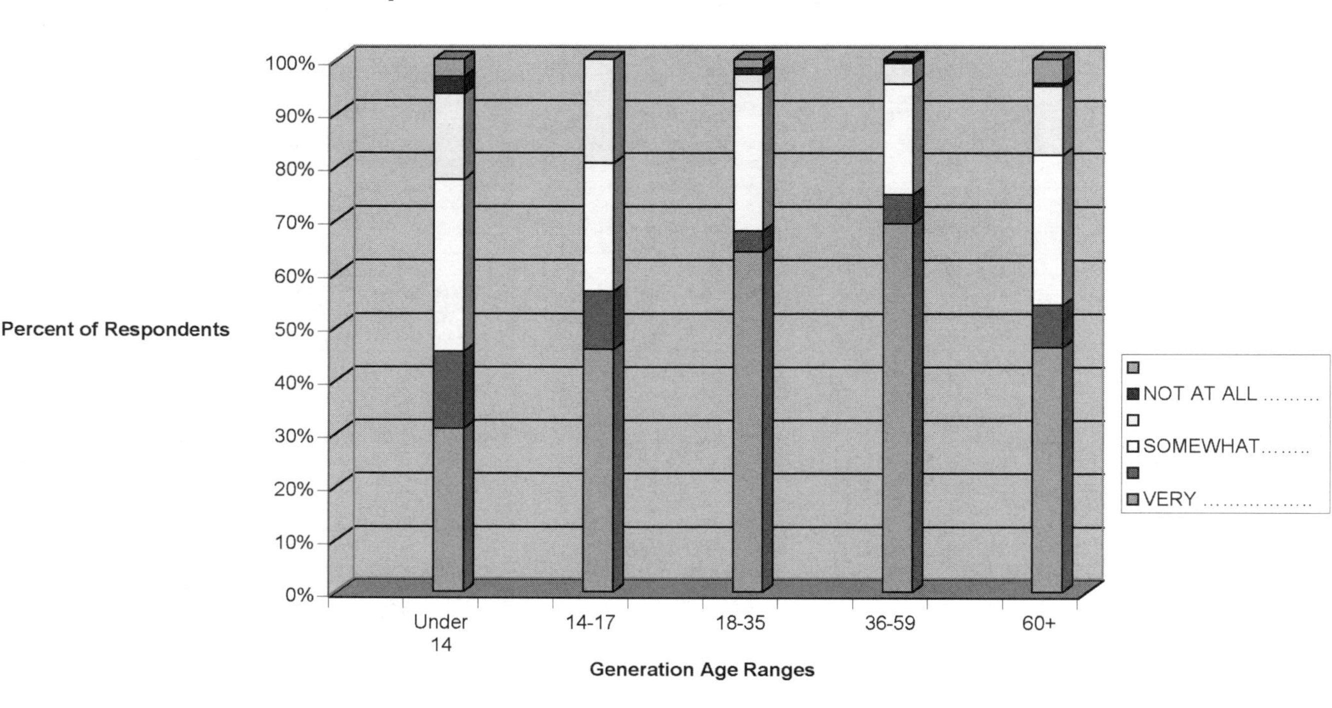

Appendix 9

Table 13: Combined Homiletic Hub Symbol Percentages

Catholic Generation Cohorts	Preacher's List of Targeted Hub Symbols Eliciting Most Responses for Each Group	St. Jerome's Total: 168 36-59: 86 60+: 35 35 & Under: 47	Washington U. Total: 250 36-59: 88 60+: 15 35 & Under: 147	St. Peter's Total: 173 36-59: 95 60+: 45 35 &Under: 33	Total % for each cohort	Total % over all cohorts
Formed Pre-	All the way;	All the way (8%)	All the way (20%)		14%	
Vatican:	Not a walk in the park	Not a walk in park (8%)			8%	
Silent	Can't edit out or jump over;		"Can't edit out or…" (26%)	"Can't edit…or jump over" (15%)	21%	23% *
and	Definition of Power	Definition of Power (74%)	Definition of Power (100%)	Definition of Power (73%)	84%	76%
Builders	Kiss of God	Kiss of God (25%)	Kiss of God (60%)	Kiss of God (42%)	43%	36%
60+	Basement of the Soul	Basement of Soul (11%)	Basement of Soul (26%)	Basement of Soul (15%)	52%	
	"fast traveling disease"			"fast-traveling disease" (4%)	4%	
	Sunday…don't get distracted and pass it up;	Sunday…don't get distracted and pass it up (34%)	Sunday…don't pass it up (40%)	Sunday…don't pass it up; (33%)	36%	40%
	"faithful connection"	"faithful connection"(45%)	faithful connection (33%)	faithful connection (22%)	34%	27%
	Surrender possessions for greater good;	Surrender possessions for greater good; (25%)	Surrender possessions for greater good; (26%)	Surrender possession for greater good (6%)	19%	
	Face of God	Face of God (5%)	Face of God (13%)	Face of God (4%)	8%	
Formed	Wireless Age of Immediacy	Wireless…Immediacy; (10%)	Wireless Age of … (35%)	Wire… Age of Immediacy; (25%)	24%	29% *
in	Tech-connection	Tech-connection (6%)	Tech-connection (37%)	Tech-connection (24%)	24%	
Vatican II:	Prison of our own making;	Prison of…own making; (10%)	Prison…our own making; (9%)	Prison of our own making; (9%)	10%	12% *
Baby Boomers	Rob time-less connected;	Rob time-less connected; (8%)	Rob time-less connection; (11%)	Rob time-less connected; (21%)	14%	
36-59	Kiss of God	Kiss of God (22%)	Kiss of God (45%)	Kiss of God (45%)	38%	
	"Preteen Niece" story	"Preteen Niece" story (6%)	"Preteen Niece" story (7%)	"Preteen Niece" story (4%)	6%	7% *
	Remote control discipleship;	Remote…discipleship; (12%)	Remote control disciple…; (38%)	Remote control disciple…; (22%)	24%	
	Perpetual Distraction	Perpetual Distraction (46%)	Perpetual Distraction (48%)	Perpetual Distraction (34%)	43%	
	Power: lunch, walk, point;	Power: lunch, walk, point; (75%)	Power: lunch, walk, point; (100%)	Power: lunch, walk, point; (85%)	87%	
	"Beam me up, Scottie"	"Beam me up" (20%)	"Beam me up" (4%)	"Beam me up" (10%)	12%	10% *
Formed after	"Beam me up"	"Beam me up" (4%)	"Beam me up" (4%)	"Beam me up" (15%)	8%	
Vat. II:	Harry Potter	Harry Potter (12%)	Harry Potter (8%)	Harry Potter (18%)	13%	
Generation X	Perpetual Distraction	Perpetual Distraction (31%)	Perpetual Distraction (60%)	Perpetual Distraction (30%)	41%	
and Millennial	Wireless fidelity		Wireless fidelity (35%)	Wireless fidelity (30%)	33%	
35 and Under	Kiss of God	Kiss of God (14%)	Kiss of God (36%)	Kiss of God (24%)	25%	
	Power of my friendship	Power of my friendship (34%)	Power of my friendship (87%)	Power of my friendship (48%)	57%	
	'I am your connection'	'I am your connection' (12%)	'I am your connection' (36%)	'I am your connection' (18%)	22%	
	Preteen Niece story	"Preteen Niece" story (4%)	"Preteen Niece" story (9%)	"Preteen Niece" story (6%)	7%	
	"At ten for IM"		"At ten for IM" (6%)	"At ten for IM" (3%)	5%	

(* = percentages figured with only two categories (23% from ages 36 and up; the bottom four from ages 59 and below)

Appendix 10

Focus Group for Fr. Andrew Carl Wisdom, O.P.
Intergenerational Preaching Project
St. Peter Parish, Kirkwood
Sunday, September 9, 2001

Participants were:
Alice: widow, 80s
Ben B. & Lyn: married couple, 70s
Jimmy & Martha: married couple, 50s
their children, Ben (17) and Amy B. (14)
Dave & Kris: married couple, 40s
their children: Katie (16) and Keith (14)
Thomas & Amy D.: married couple, 30s

What they heard and thought:

Jimmy: Palm Pilot, because he has "Pocket PC envy" from an earlier conversation in the week.

Martha: IM, because she has teenagers who use this daily

Lyn: says she's not much into technology, but this homily appealed to those who are

Ben B.: got lost with the refrigerator story

Dave: the refrigerator story made him think about how we want more and more. We are connected and have lots of power, but why?

Thomas: the refrigerator story showed how comfortable we can be in our rooms. PDAs and cell phones show that we can see others as contacts, not as people. People are the end, not the means to an end.

Kris: Beam me up, Scotty. What planet are we on?

Martha: remote control discipleship

Lyn: perpetual distraction

Jimmy: references to the gospel: tower of Legos, battle of GI Joe

Ben B.: Harry Potter, because he has read the books

Katie: Harry Potter

Amy B.: Internet

Ben: Internet

Keith: IMs and computers, since he talks to his friends that way, and now that his computer is broken, he has found other ways to use his time. Harry Potter also.

Amy D.: "If you have to have it, you no longer have it, it has you." Story about the digital thermostat in her home: she walks downstairs to set it, even though her husband says she could program it. . . . But it's easier just to walk downstairs . . .

Amy B.: cell phones, because everyone in high school has one and communicates that way, and she doesn't have one and wants one . . .

Lyn: what's the attraction with e-mail? What's wrong with picking up the phone?

Thomas: everyone in the office has Outlook on their computers, so now you can always see another person's schedule, and you can book a meeting with them even without talking to them

Lyn: was involved in Synod X (for the archdiocese, about 15 years ago) . . . we need to hear homilies that pertain to everyday life, about morals, the business world

Martha: quote from St. Bernard, "Christ is the Kiss of God."

Thomas: it's hard to kiss over e-mail?
with two small children, even in church there are many distractions . . .

Dave: living our life, not just surviving
We should live as Jesus wants, not as we are now
We have wireless communication with God

Ben B.: prayer is talking to Christ,
Christ doesn't need voice mail or e-mail; we are always connected.

Alice: isn't much into technology, had trouble hearing most of it.

Works Consulted

Allen, J. Ronald. "Preaching to Different Generations." *Encounter* 58, no. 4 (Autumn 1997) 369–400.

_______. *Preaching for Growth.* St. Louis: CBP Press, 1988.

Beaudoin, Tom. "Beginning Afresh: Gen-X Catholics." *America* 179, no. 16 (1998) 10–14.

_______. *Virtual Faith*. San Francisco: Jossey-Bass, 1998.

Bellah, Robert N., Richard Madsen, William M. Sullivan, Ann Swidler, and Stephen M. Tipton. *Habits of the Heart: Individualism and Commitment in American Life*. New York: Harper & Row, 1985.

Bishops Conference on Priestly Life and Ministry: National Committee of Catholic Bishops. *Fulfilled in Your Hearing: The Homily in the Sunday Assembly.* Washington, D.C.: United States Catholic Conference, 1982.

Booth, Tom. "Life Teen: 'A Mass That Became a Youth Ministry Movement.'" *Pastoral Music*, 24, no. 5 (June–July 2000) 21–24.

Burghardt, Walter J., S.J. *Preaching the Just Word.* New Haven: Yale University Press, 1996.

Buttrick, David. *Homiletic: Moves and Structures.* Philadelphia: Fortress Press, 1987.

Catechism of the Catholic Church, no. 1373. Washington, D.C.: United States Catholic Conference, 1994.

Collier, Mary Jane. "Cultural and Intercultural Communication Competence: Current Approaches and Directions for Future Research." *International Journal of Intercultural Relations,* no. 13 (1989) 287–302.

Conrad, Richard, O.P. *The Catholic Faith: A Dominican's Vision.* New York: Geoffrey Chapman, 1994.

Craddock, Fred B. *Overhearing the Gospel: Preaching and Teaching the Faith to Persons Who Have Already Heard.* Nashville: Abingdon, 1978.

Dart, Bob. "Generation: Shared Experiences Define Values, Viewpoints." *St. Louis Post-Dispatch* (April 9, 2001) G–1ff.

Davidson, James D., Andrea S. Williams, Richard A. Lamanna, Jan Stenftenagel, Kathleen Maas Weigert, William J. Whalen, Patricia Wittberg, S.C. *The Search for Common Ground: What Unites and Divides Catholic Americans.* Huntington, Ind.: Our Sunday Visitor, 1997.

Davies, Brian. *The Thought of Thomas Aquinas.* London: Oxford University Press, 1992.

Dickson, Peter R., and James L. Ginter. "Market Segmentation, Product Differentiation, and Marketing Strategy." *Journal of Marketing* 51, no. 2 (April 1987) 1–10.

Editorial. "The Price of Democracy." *Saint Louis Post Dispatch* (December 3, 2000).

Fatula, Mary Ann, O.P. *Thomas Aquinas: Preacher and Friend.* Collegeville: The Liturgical Press, 1993.

Foley, Leonard, O.F.M., ed. *Saint of the Day.* Cincinnati: St. Anthony Messenger Press, 1986.

Gee, J. P. *Social Linguistics and Literacies: Ideology in Discourses.* London: The Falmer Press, 1990.

Gleick, James. "Inescapably, Obsessively, Totally Connected: Life in the Wireless Age." *New York Times* (April 22, 2001) 62–67.

Haas, David. "We Don't Need Vibrant Worship 'with Youth'; We Need Vibrant Worship, Period." *Pastoral Music* 24, no. 5 (June–July 2000) 31–32, 39–42.

Hart, Richard, O.F.M.Cap. *Preaching: The Secret to Parish Revival.* Mystic, Conn: Twenty-Third Publications/Bayard, 2000.

Hicks, Dr. Rick and Kathy. *Boomers, Xers, and Other Strangers: Understanding the Generational Differences That Divide Us.* Wheaton, Ill.: Tyndale House, 1999.

Hilkert, Mary Catherine, O.P. *Naming Grace.* New York: Continuum, 1998.

________. "The Word Beneath the Words." *A Promise of Presence.* Michael Downey and Richard Fragomeni, ed. Washington, D.C.: The Pastoral Press, 1992.

Hirsch, Edward. *How to Read a Poem.* New York: Harcourt Brace, 1999.

Hoge, Dean. *Converts, Dropouts, Returnees: A Study of Religious Change among Catholics.* New York: The Pilgrim Press, 1981.

_______. "Catholic Generational Differences: Can We learn anything by identifying the specific issues of generational agreement and disargreement?" *America* (October 2, 1999) 14–17.

hooks, bell. *Teaching to Transgress Education as the Practice of Freedom*. London: Rautledge, 1994.

Johnson, Fern. *Speaking Culturally: Language Diversity in the United States.* London: Sage Publications, 2000.

Jonaitis, Dorothy, O.P. *Unmasking Apocalyptic Preaching: Cosmic Drama of Hope.* Thesis Project: Aquinas Institute of Theology, 2002.

_______. "Gospel Power: Power in the Service of Compassion." *Tessera: Dominican Life and Mission Journal* 5, no. 2 (Winter 1995) 9–11.

Lefevere, Patricia. "Theologian: GenXers Make Uneasy Peace with Church." *National Catholic Reporter* (October 6, 2000).

Lewis, Michael. "Boom Box." *The New York Times Magazine* (August 13, 2000) 38–41, 51, 65–67.

Ludwig, Robert A. *Reconstructing Catholicism for a New Generation.* New York: Crossroad, 1996.

Porter, Richard E., and Larry A. Samovar. "An Introduction to Intercultural Communication." *Intercultural Communication.* Belmont, Cal: Wadsworth Publishing, 1997.

Putnam, Todd. "Behind the Wheel and Driving the Nation's Culture." *The New York Times: Week In Review Section* (November 2000).

Reid, Barbara E., O.P., and Leslie J. Hoppe, O.F.M. *Preaching from the Scriptures: New Directions for Preparing Preachers.* Chicago: Catholic Theological Union, 1998.

Roberto, John. *Generations of Faith: Institute Program.* Omaha, Neb., May, 2000.

Romaine, Suzanne. "Language Choice" and "Language in Society/Society in Language." *Language in Society: An Introduction to Sociolinguistics.* London: Oxford University Press, 1994.

Rosen, Jay. "Playing the Primary Chords." *Harper's Magazine* (March 1992).

Ruane, Edward, O.P. "The Spirituality of the Preacher." *In the Company of Preachers.* Collegeville: The Liturgical Press, 1993.

Sacks, Jonathan. "Markets and Morals." *First Things,* no. 105 (August/September, 2000) 23–28.

Scott, Karla. "Strategies of Cultural Competence: Language Use in HIV Prevention Programs for African American Communities." Paper presented at the 127th Annual Meeting of the National Communication Association, Seattle (November 11, 2000).

Scotton, Carol Myers. "The Negotiation of Identities in Conversation: A Theory of Markedness and Code Choice." *International Journal of Social Language* 44 (1983).

Second Vatican Council. Decree on Ministry and Life of Priests, 1965. *Vatican II: The Conciliar and Postconciliar Documents.* vol. 1, newly rev. ed., Austin Flannery, O.P., ed. New York: Costello Publishing, 1996.

Smith, Wendell R. "Product Differentiation and Market Segmentation as Alternative Marketing Strategies." *Journal of Marketing* 20 (July 1956) 3–38.

Soards, Marion L. *The Apostle Paul: An Introduction to His Writings and Teaching.* New York: Paulist Press, 1987.

Spitzberg, Brian H. "Communication Competence: Measures of Perceived Effectiveness." *A Handbook for the Study of Human Communication*, Charles H. Tardy, ed. Norwood, N.J.: Ablex.

Spitzer, Alan B. "The Historical Problem of Generations." *American Historical Review* 78, no. 5 (December 1973) 1353–83.

Stendahl, Krister. *Paul among Jews and Gentiles*. Philadelphia: Fortress Press, 1976.

Strauss, William, and Neil Howe. *The Fourth Turning: An American Prophecy.* New York: Broadway Books, 1997.

_______. *13th Generation: Abort, Retry, Ignore, Fail?* New York: Vintage Books, 1993.

_______. *Generations: The History of America's Future.* New York: William Morrow, 1991.

_______. *Millennials Rising: The Next Great Generation.* New York: Vintage Books, 2000.

Trueheart, Charles. "Welcome to the Next Church." *The Atlantic Monthly* (August 1996) 37–56.

Tubbs Tisdale, Leonora. *Preaching as Local Theology and Folk Art.* Minneapolis: Fortress Press, 1997.

Turow, Joseph. *Breaking Up America*. Chicago: The University of Chicago Press, 1997.

United States Catholic Conference. *Catechism of the Catholic Faith.* New York: Doubleday, 1997.

United States Catholic Conference. *Catechism of the Catholic Church. Libreria Editrice Vaticana, Città del Vaticano*, Latin text, 1994. Mahwah, N.J.: Paulist Press, 1994.

Van Dijk, Teun A. "Discourse as Interaction in Society." *Discourse As Social Interaction.* 2. Teun A. Van Dijk, ed. London: Sage Publications, 1997.

Vann, Gerald, O.P. *The Pain of Christ and the Sorrow of God.* New York: Alba House, 1947.

Webb, Joseph M. *Preaching and the Challenge of Pluralism.* St. Louis: Chalice Press, 1998.

Wilkie, William L. "Market Segmentation." *Consumer Behavior,* 3rd ed. New York: John Wiley & Sons, 1994.

Winter, Frederick. "Marketing Segmentation: A Tactical Approach." *Marketing Manager: A Comprehensive Reader.* Jadish N. Sheth and Dennis E. Garret, ed. Cincinnati: South-Western Publishing Co., 1986.

Zimmerman, John C. "Leadership Across the Gaps Between Generations." *Crux* 31: 42–54.

Index